I'm Sober... So Now What?
UNITY IN RECOVERY

Melissa Gissy Witherspoon

World Publishing and Productions

I'm Sober... So Now What? series awards

Non Fiction: Inspiration

Non Fiction: Health & Wellness - Addiction & Recovery

Non Fiction: Self-Help - Inspiration

With gratitude, a portion of the proceeds from
the sale of this book will be given back
to the sober community through Sober-Now (501c3)

Pay it forward:
If you would like to share my message of hope
with others, scan the QR code below
to make a donation to Sober-Now.
Funds raised provide copies of this
book to recovery centers, the incarcerated,
sober living, human trafficking safe houses, and
those who cannot afford a copy.

Dedication

This book is dedicated to every person whose
life has been impacted by addiction.

Also, to my husband, Derek, and four children—
Tyler, Hailey, Caroline, and Jake.
My love for you is endless. You have inspired me to
become a better person and live a sober life.

To my family and friends who loved me and
believed in me when I did not.

And above all, I give all glory and praise to God.
For without Him, I am nothing.

Acknowledgments

A special thank you to each of the following individuals who played key roles in bringing this book to completion. Without your encouragement and prayers, this book wouldn't have come to fruition:

Dr. Gary Chapman

Victoria Harrow

Connie A. VanHorn

Kimberly Hobbs

Julie Jenkins

Kelly Williams Hale

Mary Lynn England

Rev. James Stuhrenberg

Paula Griffin

Gerald Bryant

Hank & Tina Rudge

Friends of Sober-Now

Contents

Foreword

In my years as a counselor and pastor, I have walked alongside many individuals and families whose lives have been impacted by addiction, witnessing their pain, confusion, and heartbreak. But I have also seen redemption, healing, and restored relationships when the incredible power of love has been allowed to do its transforming work.

That is why I believe deeply in the message of this book. Melissa Gissy Witherspoon writes from a place of hard-earned wisdom—wisdom forged not only through personal struggle but through the courageous choice to recover out loud in order to help others. Melissa invites us all into the vulnerable spaces of her life, not to highlight her own journey but rather to remind us that healing is possible and we don't have to walk that road alone.

Addiction isolates. It convinces us that we are unworthy of love and beyond the reach of grace. But connection—the kind of connection built on authenticity, humility, and compassion—ultimately brings us back to life. It's no coincidence that the principles found in *The 5 Love Languages* have found their way into the pages of this book. Love is not merely a feeling; it is a choice we make every day. And in recovery, it is often the choice that saves a life.

Whether you are someone walking the road of recovery, a loved one desperate to understand and support someone struggling, or simply a human being longing for deeper relationships, the truths found here will resonate deeply. Melissa shares with humility and boldness that unity is not about perfection but about presence. Unity is about sitting with one another in the hard places, offering grace when it's least expected, and believing—perhaps even before they believe it for themselves—that they are worthy of love.

In my own work, I have often said love is the most powerful force on earth, but we must express it in ways others can receive it. This is why I am encouraged to see the concept of love languages applied so beautifully to the recovery journey. In the aftermath of addiction, we must often relearn how to be in community with others, including how to love and be loved. We must discover practical, tangible ways to restore the connection, trust, and belonging that addiction seeks to destroy.

Melissa's words are an offering of hope, a call to embrace the sometimes difficult yet always miraculous process of healing—not just for those in recovery but for the entire ecosystem of relationships surrounding them. She reminds us that healing happens in community—in small acts of kindness and in the steady, daily choice to keep showing up for ourselves and each other.

My prayer is that as you turn the pages of this book, you will find more than just inspiration—you will discover a roadmap toward deeper connection, greater understanding, and renewed hope. May these words reveal that no matter where you have been or how broken your story may have left you, there is a path forward. And that path is best walked together.

It is never too late to begin again. It is never too late to choose love.

Dr. Gary Chapman
Author of *The 5 Love Languages*

A Letter to Loved Ones Impacted by Addiction

If you're reading this, chances are addiction has touched your life. To those who have watched someone you love battle this disease, as I have, know that you are not alone. The loved ones of an addict carry a heavy mix of fear, grief, guilt, anger, and helplessness. If you've experienced this firsthand, you know it's nearly impossible to explain the full weight of that emotional burden. I have walked the same path you are walking; I see you and understand that weight.

My older sister Brandy, who struggled with addiction for many years, is in prison and labeled a criminal on paper; her charges are all drug-related. But that label fails to tell the whole story. Since she was a child, crimes committed against her have defined her struggle, resulting in years of pain inflicted on her body, heart, and mind. She was just a little girl when it all began, too young to protect herself from the horrors she faced. When the world became too painful, she turned to drugs, alcohol, and anything that promised numbness.

My baby sister Amanda had a similar story, but her addiction didn't land her behind bars—it led to her tragic death. Three years ago, we lost Amanda to an accidental fentanyl overdose. It was the first time our family had experienced the loss of someone so close, and every part of it was devastating. I felt completely alone. There were very few people I felt safe enough to share Amanda's struggles with. I was ashamed. I didn't think anyone would understand.

But then I turned to Melissa, the author of this book. She listened, she showed up, and she created a space where I didn't have to carry the shame or sorrow by myself. During one of the darkest seasons of my life, Melissa reminded me that even in the aftermath of something so shattering, unity and hope are still possible.

The loss left me in agony, but my grief was just one part of the broader pain our entire family has endured. For years, we held on to hope, praying that both Brandy and Amanda would find sobriety. More often than not, though, we were left feeling helpless and heartbroken.

My family didn't always handle addiction well. I don't know many who are equipped to deal with the catastrophic scenarios it creates. My mother was caught in her own addiction, and my father tried to escape his pain by burying himself in work, often succumbing to frustration and anger. As for me, I grew up alongside my sisters, but I didn't share their addiction; instead, I ran from my problems. I chased comfort in the wrong places and people, hoping to find a life that could erase my childhood pains.

I attempted countless times to reach my sisters over the years, clinging to hope while encouraging and pleading with them to choose a better path. I became angry when they would steal from me or lie to me. I can now see that they felt a pain much deeper than I could understand. Recently, I came across Amanda's diary, which she kept before her death while battling addiction. She wanted to change; she longed to be free from the disease and sought freedom for those around her who were reaping the consequences of her actions. What stood out the most was her loneliness in the struggle.

I wish I had known then what I now understand about addiction. I wish I realized that unity and connection are powerful forces in healing and sobriety. I wish I had been able to see, with eyes of compassion, the pain and heartbreak that often ushers in and fuels the disease of addiction. But rather than sitting in regrets of my past, I choose to share a part of my story with you in hopes that you will be inspired to reach out to support groups and welcome connection to help you navigate your pain and struggles. To find ways to love the addict in your life while also setting healthy boundaries.

We need unity—not isolation or separation—to overcome addiction. Loving someone in active addiction is heavy and can feel unbearable. It doesn't just weigh down those who suffer from it, but it drags their loved ones down with them. Addiction strikes in cunning, baffling ways. But true change can begin when we start to understand what addiction really is and recognize how essential unity is in the journey of recovery.

Unity was missing during my sisters' struggles; that absence kept my family from truly supporting one another. Please hear me: Hope and healing begin when we come together as a community. I didn't want Amanda to die. I wish she were here today, standing beside me in this call to action. But even in her absence, miracles have unfolded through unity. Opportunities like this—our connection through this book—keep her memory alive. Knowing that her life, though cut far too short, can still be a source of hope for others brings me peace.

At Amanda's funeral, I shared about her life, God's redeeming love, and the hope we hold through faith in something greater than ourselves. Her celebration of life became an opportunity to promote unity among those who attended. We witnessed many miracles that day. Several people surrendered their burdens at the altar. Amanda used to say, "If one life is changed by mine, then I guess it counted." Amanda's life counted. Your life counts. And your loved one's life counts.

My sisters were hurting. Addiction provided them with a false sense of comfort—a contrived and harmful way to escape from all their pain and suffering that eventually shattered everything and everyone around them. And once they were in that cycle of insanity, isolation from all corners of our family unit grew. But that doesn't have to be your story.

What if we choose unity instead of fighting alone? It might be one of the hardest things we do—but also one of the most healing. Because when we lean into connection, shame starts to lose its grip. And that's where real change begins.

That's what this book is about. We don't have to face addiction alone. When we lead with love instead of judgment, even the darkest struggles can give way to recovery. Don't let the chains of addiction or resentment toward someone who took that path hold you back. There is freedom for all of us, and it begins in unity. There is a community waiting to walk this road with you; may you find them.

Melissa and I co-authored the anthology *Faith Unchained: Climbing to Freedom by God's Grace.* After you've read this book, I encourage you to read the stories in it, many of which were written by women who have overcome addiction. I believe it will offer you insight and hope for restoration in your and your loved one's life.

I'm honored to connect with you through these words. I will be praying for you and your loved ones to experience breakthrough, one day at a time, in perfect unity.

Connie VanHorn
Co-Author of *Hope Alive* and *Faith Unchained*
In loving memory of Amanda M. VanHorn
(June 26, 1983 - June 17, 2022)

Introduction

W hether you are at the beginning stages of your recovery journey, have been walking this path for a while, or are a loved one of someone who has been impacted by substance use disorder—better known as addiction—I want you to know one thing from the very beginning: You are not alone.

This is the second book in the *I'm Sober... So Now What?* series. In the first, *I'm Sober... So Now What? A Journey of Hope and Healing*, I shared the truth of where I came from—my journey through the heartbreak and devastation of substance use disorder into the beautiful, sometimes still messy, but always miraculous process of healing. I opened my heart and shared how God divinely met me at my rock bottom, empowering me to rebuild my life from the inside out and discover a purpose that's so much bigger than myself.

My hope in sharing the struggle and victory of my past was to help answer the questions of those in danger of being swept away by this disease. Understanding the depth of pain created by addiction can be a lifeline for the one watching their loved one drowning, the one presently caught in the current, and the one successfully battling the undertow and searching for a new way to live. My story offers hope—and don't we all need hope? Along the way, I learned that sharing our stories is how we remind each other that the struggle is real and that we are not the only ones going through it.

This book, the second in the series, is about what comes next after we have stopped the drug of choice that prohibited us from any chance of truly living—the "So Now What?" It's about connection, unity, and the quiet strength that comes when we begin to heal—not just as individuals but together. I didn't write this book only for those who are in recovery. It's also for the mothers, fathers, siblings, partners, and friends—the ones who have loved through the chaos and have been left desperate and shattered through the silence. Every person in active addiction and recovering from it has an entire ecosystem surrounding them—they need healing, too. My hope is that these pages will help bridge the gap and create a space for compassion and better understanding. That together, we might find a new way to walk forward.

Why do I feel called to focus on unity? Because the disease of addiction thrives in isolation. It whispers, "No one will understand what you're going through," "You are too far gone," and "You can manage this on your own." Those lies are the fuel perpetuating a cycle of insanity. Imagine being on fire; in a desperate attempt to put out the flames, you grab what you think is a container filled with water, but it turns out to be full of gasoline. That's what isolation does. We reach for it, thinking it will quiet the chaos, but instead, it fuels the very fire we're trying to escape. Connection, on the other hand, is like a blanket—it smothers the flames and cuts off the oxygen that keeps the blaze alive. It gives us a fighting chance against the fiery furnace of addiction.

Healing happens in community. It happens when we reach out and realize someone is reaching back. It happens when we share our stories, let others see the *real* us, and allow ourselves to be loved—exactly as we are.

I've walked the path of recovery alone, and I have walked it in unity with others. When I tried to do it alone, the weight was too much to bear. The silence and loneliness pulled me back down, and unfortunately, relapse was inevitable. Sadly...multiple relapses. But this last time around, when I leaned into connection—when I opened up to community, to support, and to a power greater than myself whom I call God—that's when the true healing began.

Faith is a fundamental human experience that involves believing in the truth of something, even if there isn't complete proof or understanding. When I started my search for a connection to something greater than myself, I was confused, even overwhelmed by the entire concept of that. My life had been led by ego, and my self-will had run rampant for so long that the thought of changing lanes and handing over the wheel to let someone else drive seemed impossible. You know that song "Jesus, Take the Wheel"? That was not a song I was willing to sing along with. But as I dove deeper into recovery through a 12-step program, a spiritual awakening unfolded—one that led me into a personal relationship with my Higher Power. Steadily, over time, that connection has become the very core of my recovery.

Unity and connection didn't just help me stay clean and sober—they became the foundation of my long-term recovery. Nearly twelve years later, without a single relapse, I can say with all my sober heart: the difference this time is connection. I didn't come this far because I had everything figured out. I came this far because I finally let people in and trusted the One who does have the answers. I surrendered fully. I leaned into faith, surrounded myself with community, and began to believe that even the broken parts of my story carried purpose. When I say I leaned into faith, some days this was the most difficult challenge of all, and quite frankly, some days it still is.

I understand many of us in recovery have been hurt by religion. "Church hurt" is a real thing. Sometimes, the walls go up as soon as the "G" word is mentioned or the topic of faith enters the conversation. I get it. For years, that was my response, too. That's why I invite you—gently—to stick with me. To read my words for what they are: A shared experience. An offering, if you will. An opportunity to express what I've learned in hopes that something in it speaks to you. My intent is not to change your path but to help you walk the one best designed for you. At the end of the day, we're all after the same thing: a better way of life. My prayer is simple: May this book help you get there.

On my healing journey, I have met so many others whose paths looked different than mine. It's like a big, beautiful melting pot—people choosing different methods, coming from different beliefs, but all moving toward the same purpose: freedom from addiction. In these pages, you'll read about some of those connections, and you'll discover ways you can connect with them as well.

As you turn the pages, you will find pieces of my story—personal reflections, insights, and tools that can help you build deeper connections in every area of your recovery. Have you ever heard of *The 5 Love Languages*? There's even a chapter in this book that applies Dr. Gary Chapman's world-renowned framework to recovery.

Why did I feel so strongly that Dr. Chapman's work should be integrated into this book? Because after years of not knowing how to love or be loved, many of us need a starting point. We require practical ways to rebuild what addiction tried to take from us— the ability to give and receive love in healthy, meaningful ways. Dr. Chapman agreed to apply his concept because he believes that, with work and commitment, addiction can be overcome and that everyone in this world deserves to love and be loved.

I invite you to join me through the next pages of discovery. Let's take the first steps together to build connection, creating a life worth living. Find a cozy spot, settle in, and by the time you close the pages of this book, I pray you will be inspired to be led by the truth that you are not alone on your journey and that life after addiction is attainable and more beautiful than you can imagine. We are in this together, growing and walking a path of freedom from addiction in unity, one day at a time.

Welcome to *I'm Sober... So Now What?: Unity in Recovery*. I am grateful you are here.

CHAPTER ONE

Unity Found in the Soil of Surrender

"In the garden of unity, every flower blooms with its own unique beauty, yet all are nourished by the same soil."
—Abdu'l-Bahá

There's a theory that says connection is the opposite of addiction. And while it may sound simple, it's anything but that. This truth reaches the heart of what it means to heal. Healing is not just stopping destructive behaviors; healing is reclaiming your place in the human story. It is remembering that you were never meant to do life alone.

Addiction doesn't just survive in isolation—it thrives there. It grows in the dark corners where shame echoes loudest, guilt piles up like bricks, and loneliness convinces you that no one could possibly understand. Over time, you stop reaching out... and, eventually, stop believing anyone would reach back.

That's what happened to me. I lived in that place for over twenty years—cut off from others, buried beneath the rubble of my own choices. I didn't just lose relationships; I lost the belief that I even deserved them. And without connection, I slowly disappeared from myself.

In my first book, *I'm Sober... So Now What?: A Journey of Hope and Healing*, I shared about a pivotal moment that marked the beginning of my real surrender—the moment I hit rock bottom on the cold, hard floor of my unfinished basement. That day my idea of surrender looked a lot like giving up. I didn't fall to my knees in praise; I collapsed in defeat. I begged God to let me die. I wasn't looking for healing. I was looking for an end to years of pain.

But what I received instead was a vision. A grace of clarity in a glimpse of something greater than myself. I went from pleading for death to realizing deep in my soul that I was meant to live. That there was purpose in my story. That, just maybe, everything I had survived wasn't meant to bury me but to become the soil from which something new could grow.

That revelation didn't instantly make everything better. There was no thunderclap erasing the years of pain and destruction that the poor choices I made through my addiction had caused. But it did give me the strength to say yes to the next right thing, which was going away to treatment again. This time to a dual diagnosis treatment facility, where I would spend months away from my family, my friends, and everything familiar as I faced the layers of trauma, dysfunction, and chaos that had built up over the course of more than two decades.

This wasn't my first attempt at recovery. There had been many times I tried to get sober, to clean up the mess, to become someone

I could stand living with. But I had never fully surrendered. I was willing to give up drinking but would not address the deeper patterns. Willing to let go of drugs, but not the need to control everything around me. I was willing to stop lying but not willing to open up and tell the truth about what really happened—the truth about what lived at the root of my addiction. Those measures of halfway efforts always led to relapse. And with each relapse came more guilt and shame.

I treated recovery like trimming weeds, never digging deep enough to pull out the rotten roots. And I had learned the hard way that weeds always grow back stronger when you only deal with what's on the surface.

So there I was, physically sober, emotionally raw, and spiritually bankrupt in a treatment facility hundreds of miles from home, where I was finally ready to talk about what I never wanted to speak out loud. I talked about the trauma. The physical abuse. The sexual abuse. The shame. The secrets. I started whispering the things that had silenced me for years.

To me, surrender meant weakness. I was never going to be caught waving a white flag. I was not someone who surrendered; I was a fighter. And when I wasn't fighting, I was running. But that day in the basement, I had no fight left. And I couldn't run anymore. All I had left was a choice: surrender or die.

I didn't surrender just the obvious things, like the substances or the chaos. I started turning toward the quieter, more hidden parts of myself—the ones I kept locked away out of shame or fear.

Sometimes I had to walk through the process more than once before I could be fully honest, but with each layer shed, something in me shifted. And eventually, something rooted.

That's when I began to understand that surrender isn't weakness—it's the most courageous kind of strength. It's saying, "I'm tired of carrying this alone," and being brave enough to set it down. And what surprised me most was when I surrendered I didn't fall apart; instead, I began to find unity. As I opened up, others stepped in—counselors, recovery group members, and even strangers. Suddenly, I wasn't alone anymore. I was connected soul-deep, not surface-level. And that connection became the soil where healing could finally begin to grow. Surrender made that kind of deep healing possible. And surrender made unity possible.

Unity is what has kept me alive since that day on the basement floor. It's what has sustained me through nearly twelve years of sobriety. It's what has allowed me to love deeply, to parent mindfully, to serve faithfully, and to walk intentionally with others as they uncover their own soil of surrender.

And here is something profound I have learned along the way: Surrender isn't a one-time movement; it's a rhythm we return to again and again. In recovery, each new season brings new invitations to let go of things we were never meant to carry—old fears, false identities, the urge for control. And every time we choose to surrender, we make space for something new to take root.

Every challenge we face becomes an opportunity for deeper growth. Deeper connection. With others, yes, but also with our Creator. And through that connection, something powerful happens: we begin to experience unity, not only with the world around us but within ourselves. A quiet wholeness that says, *This is who I am, and this is where I belong.*

Recovery is about so much more than avoiding a substance. It's about rebuilding the emotional and spiritual ties that addiction severed. It's about finding your way back to community, to love, to a life that feels worth living again. When we connect with others, we don't just survive—we thrive. And as we move forward, we start to believe a new story about ourselves: one where we are seen, known, and loved despite the chapters we'd rather erase.

Connection is the soil where healing takes root. It's where the old, false narratives begin to lose their grip. In the presence of real connection, we remember the truth: we were made for belonging.

And when we step back into that connection, something beautiful begins to unfold. We start to remember who we are—that we're worthy of love, that we're not too far gone, and that we were created for more than just surviving.

Recovery grows in community, and healing happens in the company of others. Whether it's through a support group, a 12-step program, volunteering, attending church, spending time with a trusted friend, or even having a conversation with a stranger who listens without judgment—connection becomes the bridge back to life.

It is important to understand that unity doesn't mean sameness. It means we are connected by something greater than our individual struggles. We are connected by love, grace, and purpose. In that unity, we find the strength to grow into who we were always meant to become. And the source that feeds that growth is within each interaction we have with one another.

Here's the thing about growth—it's rarely instant. Most of the time, it's slow and quiet. So quiet that we don't even realize it's happening until one day, something inside us feels different.

Think of a seed. Before it can grow, the soil has to be prepared. That means turning it over, breaking it open, softening what's become hard and compacted. That's what surrender does. It breaks up the old ground—our secrets, our shame, our survival tactics—and makes space for something new to take root.

And here's what's incredible: that seed already holds everything it needs for life, beauty, and fruit. But it won't grow just because it exists. It has to be planted. Then, it needs time. It needs the right environment—nourishment, care, light. And it needs to stay rooted, even when the conditions aren't perfect.

Whether you're walking through recovery yourself or loving someone who is, that seed has already been planted. The potential to grow—to heal, to bloom, to thrive—is already inside of you. But where you choose to plant yourself matters.

If we keep showing up in the same toxic environments, around people who keep us stuck, we stay small. But when we plant ourselves in healthy soil—surrounded by truth, love, and people who believe in us—we begin to thrive.

And here's the most beautiful part: growth doesn't stop with us.

Like a dandelion in the wind, once we bloom, our healing carries seeds. With one gust, those seeds scatter—some landing nearby, some traveling far. And each one holds the power to start new life in someone else's soil.

That's how connection continues.

Growth takes time. Unity doesn't bloom overnight—but every small act of courage, every step toward connection, plants a seed for something greater.

Keep showing up. Keep turning the soil. Keep planting seeds in fertile ground and watch how unity begins to bloom from the soil of your surrender.

Reflection

What if the breakthrough you've been waiting for isn't found in doing more, but in letting go? Sometimes, the bravest thing we can do is release the grip of fear and control and simply surrender to the possibility of something new. You don't have to have it all figured out. You don't have to feel completely ready. You only have to be willing to take one small, courageous step, trusting that grace will meet you there. Maybe surrender looks like opening your heart to connection, even if it feels risky. Perhaps it's allowing yourself to be seen without the mask of perfection. Or maybe as simple as whispering, "I can't do this alone, and I don't have to."

Every seed planted in the soil of surrender holds the promise of new life. So, breathe deep and settle into your roots, knowing that surrender isn't weakness—it's nourishment for your soul.

When you release what's been holding you back, you make room for the light to pour in. And in that light, you will grow.

CHAPTER TWO

Better Together

"We are not meant to journey alone. Every heart we meet is a
companion on the road to becoming."
—Morgan Harper Nichols

Have you ever tried to move a couch by yourself? You push and pull, huffing and puffing, trying to wedge it through a doorway that suddenly feels a whole lot smaller than you remember. You scrape the walls, bang your knuckles, and if you're anything like me, you probably say a few things under your breath that you regret later. Sure, with enough effort, you might eventually wrestle it into place. But by the time you're done, you're frustrated, exhausted, and wondering why you didn't ask for someone to help.

Life feels like that sometimes, doesn't it? And recovery? Well, recovery can feel exactly the same.

As I write this chapter, I am living that lesson out loud. I'm in the thick of co-authoring an anthology project with twenty-six incredible, spirit-led women called *Faith Unchained: Climbing to Freedom by God's Grace.* Our schedules are hectic, our Zoom calls are full of laughter and deep connections, and sometimes, there are moments when someone's vulnerability brings the whole group to tears. Together, we're building something beautiful, something bigger than any of us could have created on our own. Something that will connect us with readers worldwide.

Sure, I'm technically a lead on this book, but let me be the first to tell you—every woman involved is playing a significant role. We each have different personalities and have been shaped by various backgrounds and stories, resulting in a beautiful panorama of life. Yet, with all that diversity comes its own set of challenges.

Teamwork is not always easy. Some days, my desire for control and perfection creeps in, and I feel it would be simpler just to complete the project myself. But despite the difficulties of working with so many women, gathering them away from their busy schedules and guiding them to focus on the many steps needed to achieve success together, I still find the greatest joy in our unity. Although my leadership must keep time with the project's unique rhythm, our work together is fruitful, and I find myself smiling at the beauty of it all—the challenges and joys that come from creating something with others. It is a blessing when people come together to work for something greater than themselves.

At the same time I have been spearheading that project, I've also been writing *this* book—the one you're holding in your hands—as a solo project. I'm writing it alone in the stillness of late nights and the early hush of mornings before the world wakes up. I'm stealing moments in my car during my son's baseball practices and scribbling notes while sitting in drive-thru lines and grocery store parking lots.

Some things in life are meant to be carried alone for a season—the quiet callings, the soul work, the projects that ask us to wrestle with the page, the heart, and our own reflection. Like me writing this book in those early mornings and late nights, some journeys require us to walk a solitary path.

But even in those solo endeavors, we are not untouched by community.

Because while the writing may be mine, the refining is shared. A proofreader's careful eye, an editor's wisdom, a friend's timely encouragement, and always—always—the quiet guidance of the Creator. This is unity, too. Not loud or crowded, but gently woven through each step.

This book is personal. It's deeply meaningful to me to have the opportunity to connect and share my experiences with you as others have with me. But it feels heavy at times. Carrying something on your own will do that to you.

I've often wondered, *Why does the anthology—despite the extra effort and complexity—feel lighter and more joyful? Why does it fill me up, while working alone on this book sometimes feels like such a slow and solitary climb?*

The answer settled into my heart with such clarity it nearly took my breath away.

We aren't meant to do life alone.

From the very beginning, we were designed for connection.

Truth be told, this hasn't been an easy lesson for me to learn. When I started my writing journey a few years ago, I fought it every step of the way. I felt that familiar tug in my spirit to write, and instead of answering the call, I did everything I could to avoid it. I ignored it. I rationalized my way out of it. And when the call just wouldn't stop pressing on my heart, I finally gave in—but not because I felt inspired. Quite frankly, I was hesitant because I felt unqualified and was annoyed at the entire idea of being asked to do something I didn't believe I could do.

I thought, *Fine. I'll just write the book, check the box, and maybe this nagging feeling will finally leave me alone.*

But God had something entirely different in mind.

From my one very reluctant "yes," a book to help others find hope and healing was born; from that, a nonprofit blossomed. Connections I never expected began to form in every direction. Doors opened that I didn't even know existed. Looking back now, I can see how every step was woven into a bigger design—one I couldn't understand at the time but was perfectly laid out by the hands of a God who knew exactly where I was headed.

It turns out that all I really needed to do was show up and then keep showing up as I followed His will, not mine.

Even after eleven years of recovery, I still wrestle with obedience. I still catch myself questioning, resisting, and trying to control the outcome before even taking the first step. But if there's anything this journey has taught me, it's that perfection isn't the goal. Progress is. And no matter how difficult things seem or how unqualified we feel, what matters most is that we just keep showing up and making our best effort each day.

The most surprising part of all this is where that willingness to show up has led me.

Never in my life did I think I'd become someone who regularly flips through the pages of a Bible. That wasn't my story. That wasn't my plan. But it didn't start with some grand moment of revelation. It started small, and really, it started in secret.

At first, I would flip through the pages, land my finger on a random spot, and read whatever verse I happened to be pointing to. I wasn't looking for some structured Bible study. I was just dipping my toes in, testing the waters, wondering if maybe there really was something there for me.

And every time—without fail—the words I needed seemed to find me.

Stories written centuries ago about people whose lives looked nothing like mine somehow spoke directly into my situation.

I didn't tell anyone at first. This exploration felt too fragile to share. Quietly, I ordered a simple Bible off Amazon—nothing fancy, just something I could open up when no one was looking.

Instead of turning to the things I usually would have—temporary distractions I chased in my past—I found myself reaching for those thin, sacred pages, wondering if I might find some real guidance for once.

And that's when I stumbled across the story of a man named Paul.

At first, I wasn't sure what to think of him. This man was fiery, intense, and more than a little wild. But as I kept reading, something in me started to recognize a familiar struggle.

Paul lived his life fully convinced he was right—until he wasn't. He made choices he later wasn't proud of, pridefully standing for power and control until he found himself completely undone by a love he hadn't understood and a grace he didn't expect and couldn't earn. The love of God through Jesus Christ—the very man he had been persecuting others for following.

After his powerful, life-changing encounter with God, though on a new path, Paul didn't walk his journey alone. He traveled with others who supported and upheld him.

Barnabas stood up for Paul when no one else trusted his transformation. Young Timothy walked closely as Paul mentored and poured his heart into him, and they grew in faith together. And then there was Silas, Paul's friend who sat in prison chains right beside him, singing hymns through the darkest nights when freedom felt impossible.

Paul understood the power of community because he relied on others to live out the purposeful life he was called to. That's why he wrote so often and so passionately about unity. He reminded the early churches that although it's easy to divide and argue, it is far more powerful—and far more holy—to stand together. He spoke about the kind of love that binds people through every hardship and refuses to give up even when things feel chaotic and hard.

And as I read his words, I couldn't help but wonder: *If even Paul needed that kind of connection, how much more do we?*

And then something else started to click for me.

It wasn't just the Bible I found myself drawn to. It was every book I read: autobiographies, testimonies, and anthologies filled with real, raw stories of people overcoming impossible odds.

I realized those books weren't just about one person's journey. They were a culmination of events and moments that included interactions with many people. No one's story was ever just about them. Their transformation happened through community, through connection, and through the lives they touched along the way.

And when you really think about it, isn't that true for all of us?

Our own lives are the same way. Sure, there will be seasons, especially early in recovery, when it feels like we're walking completely alone. That isolation is terrifying. I've lived it. Sometimes it still sneaks up on me. And for someone like me, with deep abandonment wounds, it's easy to fall back into that old thought pattern—the one that whispers, "You're all alone, and you always will be."

But are we ever truly alone? Or is that just a mindset we slip into during our most difficult moments?

The truth is, even on the loneliest days, our lives are still woven together with others.

Even if I had zero close friends, I'd still interact with people—I'd go to the grocery store, roll through a drive-thru for a sausage biscuit (because, let's be honest, I'm not passing up a good sausage biscuit), or park at a local park and go for a walk to get my steps in. And like most of us, I'd still have to show up to work, and most jobs don't happen in total isolation.

We are never really as alone as we feel.

That sense of isolation is a trick our minds play, often rooted in old hurts and patterns we're working so hard to break. It's the voice that tries to pull us back into the shadows when life is calling us out into the light.

So, no matter where you are in your day—whether you're making small talk with a cashier, smiling at someone passing by, or holding the door open for a stranger—every one of those moments is an opportunity for connection.

Maybe the people you interact with in passing aren't deep, life-long relationships, but they're still people, and those moments matter. The way we interact with every person we come across matters. If you think about it, we're like one massive, living, breathing fiber optic network—all moving through this world, crossing paths, lighting each other up in ways we don't even fully realize.

And while it's easy to focus on the positive connections, we can't ignore the other side.

What about those connections that annoy us? The people we cross paths with who just make our skin crawl? I'm sure you know exactly what I'm talking about. There isn't a person alive who gets along perfectly with everyone they meet. That's just life.

But here's the thing—those people are important, too.

They're part of our connection story, not just our connection with them but with ourselves.

How do we respond to those less-than-positive connections? At the end of the day, how does our emotional inventory balance? Would we want to be spoken to the way we've spoken to others? Are we left with amends to make? Those difficult interactions open a wide space for accountability and growth.

I borrow the phrase, "iron sharpens iron," but sometimes our growth feels more like nails on a chalkboard. Is it pleasant? No, not necessarily. But the sharpening achieved from successfully navigating those challenging moments is often the very thing that propels us to the next level in recovery.

When we use those opportunities to respond differently—to choose grace over bitterness, to hold our tongue instead of lashing out, to see the humanity in the person standing before us even when they test every nerve we have—that's where real growth happens.

There's something incredibly rewarding about coming through a less-than-ideal situation and realizing you have handled it with more grace than ever before. That feeling motivates you to keep pushing through the next hard thing and the next uncomfortable conversation. And even more gratifying, some of those conflicting relations, when worked through with compassion and grace, become our strongest connections and friendships. There are several people now firmly rooted in my life whose initial interactions could have ended in a stalemate. My choice to handle situations differently than I had in my past, trusting a deeper understanding and accepting that those people were some of my greatest blessings, opened doors I didn't know were there. And now, those situations have given me some of my dearest friends.

So even when the road feels solitary, remember—there's a difference between walking alone and being alone. Help may not always carry the load for you, but it can steady your hands, clear your vision, and remind you that even the heaviest burdens become lighter when we invite others to walk alongside us. Because at the end of the day, we're all just trying to find our way in this world. And no matter how challenging it looks, it really is better when we do it together. Somehow, this unseen unity has the power to polish the simplest tasks and make possible the challenges that once felt immovable.

Reflection

Who has brushed against the edges of your life lately? Whose presence felt like sunlight... and whose felt like sandpaper against your soul? Without trying to fix or explain it away, simply wonder: What if both were meant for your becoming? Could it be that every encounter—welcomed or unwelcome—is a thread in the tapestry, gently pulling you toward wholeness?

Let that settle. And when the next face crosses your path, take a long, slow breath and ask yourself, "What beauty might be hidden in this moment, even if it comes wrapped in discomfort?"

Then, just for a heartbeat, stay open enough to receive a voice of discernment—a gift of grace through the unity of the Holy Spirit.

CHAPTER THREE

Unity Is the Heartbeat of Recovery

*"Our human compassion binds us the one to the other—not in
pity or patronizingly, but as human beings who have learned how
to turn our common suffering into hope for the future."*
—Nelson Mandela

There have been so many times in my life when it felt like the ground was shifting underneath me, and I wasn't sure if I was standing still or slowly sinking. Most people know that feeling, even if they don't always talk about it—that quiet ache of not knowing how to fix your life but registering deep down that you can't stay where you are.

For a long time, I thought the safest thing I could do was to pull away. I figured life would hurt a little less if I could just get smaller, quieter, or less noticeable. That maybe if I stayed hidden long enough, the storms would pass over me. But hiding never saved me. It only left me lonelier as walls formed around the very places where I needed bridges.

It wasn't until I started showing up for others that I recognized that we don't experience healing when we hide. Healing happens when we risk being seen. It happens when we reach out, even if our hands are still shaking. We heal by offering love, even when we feel like we have nothing left to give.

Somewhere along the way, I realized that service isn't just a good idea or something nice to put on a checklist. It's the way we survive. It's the way we heal. Unity is the heartbeat of recovery, and service is how we keep that heart beating strong. Each time we show up for someone else or reach across the distance with open hands instead of closed fists, we breathe a little more life into our own recovery. Serving others is not just about giving; it's about being connected to something bigger than ourselves. We were never meant to walk without that connection.

I didn't understand any of that when I first found myself sitting in DUI Court, staring at a long list of requirements I wasn't sure I could meet. I had just gotten out of inpatient treatment, and now I was court-ordered to complete counseling, random drug tests, therapy, endless AA and NA meetings, and hundreds of hours of community service. And because I was a habitual violator for driving under the influence, they had revoked my driver's license for two full years. No appeals. No exceptions.

I remember sitting there, listening to the judge, and thinking, *Sure thing, Your Honor. I'll just hop on my invisible broomstick and fly myself all over town like some sober Harry Potter. Sounds doable.*

I had absolutely no idea how I was going to pull off all that was required. No car to get me around, no license even if I somehow came up with a car, and barely a dollar to my name. As for a plan—that was just wishful thinking dressed up as hope. On top of everything, whatever trust my family had left in me was hanging by a thread. The road before me felt impossible to travel before I could even take the first step.

Some days, I was crushed by the weight of it all. I wanted to sit down right where I was and quit. I wondered if maybe I was too broken to be worth saving.

But deep down, a small, stubborn flicker kept whispering, "Find a way. Show up anyway."

So I did.

I begged for rides from people who barely knew me. I walked in the rain to meetings. I stood outside recovery clubhouses, hoping someone would offer me a lift home. I sat on cold curbs after court dates, feeling like the last kid waiting for a parent who might not come.

It wasn't glamorous, and most days, it wasn't easy. But it was the beginning of something I didn't even realize I was building—a life rooted in showing up humbly, one imperfect step at a time.

And somewhere in the middle of that chaotic beginning, something started to change. Each time I showed up, even when it would have been easier to disappear, I found people who saw me before I could even see myself.

Each time I listened to the still, small voice within—even when I couldn't speak my truth—I found peace in the silence.

Each time I stayed, even when shame screamed at me to leave, I found that I was never really alone—not then, not ever.

Those early Alcoholics Anonymous (AA) meetings weren't just a box I needed to check off for DUI Court anymore. They became oxygen. They became home. In those rooms, nobody cared how many times I had fallen. They cared that I got back up. They cared that I was willing to go to any lengths to show up.

And somehow, for the first time in a long time, just being "Melissa"—no mask, no excuses—was enough.

Sitting in those plastic chairs surrounded by bad coffee and beautiful brokenness, I started to believe something my heart had been desperate to know: we heal together, or we don't heal at all.

Unity isn't optional. It's the heartbeat of recovery. Without it, we stay stuck in the old lies that tell us we're too far gone. With it, we realize we were never beyond saving.

I began to understand this concept more fully outside the rooms of recovery. Part of my sentence included hundreds of hours of community service. At first, it felt like punishment—another requirement, another hoop to jump through. The victim mentality was still very present in my first few years of getting sober.

But life has a funny way of flipping what feels like punishment into purpose.

Through community service, I found more people like me. People who were trying to rebuild something out of the ashes.

I helped clean 12-step meeting clubhouses. I stocked food pantries. I showed up for recovery walks and small events where nobody was keeping score, but everybody was quietly cheering each other on.

At some point, I stopped counting my required service hours and started planting seeds of growth in my life.

Community service connected me to people who didn't just understand my story—they became part of it. It rooted me in a new way of living—one where love isn't earned; it is simply given. One where service isn't about obligation; it is about gratitude.

And I didn't stop when the court said I could. I didn't want to.

As time went on, I started Sober-Now, an online community where I could reach others who felt as lost and scared as I once had. This movement eventually turned into a nonprofit where I am able to share hope through ministry worldwide.

I began writing a column called Recovery Reflections for *Voice of Truth* magazine, pouring pieces of my journey into words in hopes that it would help even one person believe that change was possible.

I've met people through recovery spaces—real people with real scars—who have become like family as we've grown and served together, like those at The Hope Shot, with whom I've partnered to do outreach across states and digital spaces. Together, we've reached people we might never have met but who we knew mattered. Some of the women I met online—content creators like Rachel from Addict with Purpose and Sonya Johnson—became not just content creator collaborators but true sisters in recovery and instrumental in my faith journey. Many wrote in *Faith*

Unchained with me, sharing stories stitched together by God's grace.

Every friendship, every collaboration, and every act of service kept weaving one sacred truth deeper into my heart: Unity is the heartbeat of recovery. Without it, I never would have made it. With it, I am more alive than I ever thought possible.

Looking back now, it almost takes my breath away to realize how much goodness started with something so small—one scared girl, one broken prayer, and one stubborn decision to keep showing up when it would have been easier not to.

Healing didn't happen all at once. It happened in quiet, unseen ways. In the lift of a hand. In the opening of a door. In the shaky offering of love when I didn't feel worthy to give it.

And what I found is this: You don't have to have it all together to make a positive change. You just have to be willing to show up. Show up even when life gets complicated and it's hard to keep going. Show up when everything inside you says you have nothing left to give. When you do, you will realize that just being you is enough. That's the moment everything will start to shift in the right direction; you will begin to fully understand that what other people need is the real, authentic you, not some polished version.

Our suffering in active addiction is not a life sentence; it is a doorway to connection, a chance to turn our most challenging moments into hope for someone else's future. Service became the bridge between my brokenness and my healing, and unity kept me walking across it. Every time I reached out a trembling hand, someone stronger held it. And one day, almost without realizing it, I became that stronger hand for someone else. That's the heartbeat of recovery—the sacred rhythm of giving and receiving, falling and being lifted, standing together in the light after so many years lost in the dark. And the most beautiful truth is that the heartbeat of recovery lives in each of us, steady and strong, waiting for the moment we decide to carry it forward.

Reflection

Healing happens in the small, often unseen places—in the moments we risk connection when it would feel safer to hide. Service and unity aren't distant goals; they're lifelines you can grab hold of right now. You don't have to wait until you feel ready or worthy—healing begins the moment you take that first shaky step toward connection. In reaching out, you'll find that hope and purpose often meet you right where you are.

So, ask yourself: Where am I still hiding, and what small step can I take to show up—for myself or someone else? You don't need to see the whole path ahead. Just take the next step. That's where healing begins and where the heartbeat of recovery starts to grow stronger through you.

CHAPTER FOUR

A Seat at the Table

"We should all have a seat at the table. And if there isn't one, we should build a bigger table."
—Unknown

When I first stumbled into recovery, I believed connection would only be found with those who bore the same battle scars. That the only people who could walk alongside me were those who had fallen into the depths and clawed their way back toward the light. I didn't realize that a seat had already been prepared for me—in rooms I hadn't yet dared to enter, in communities I didn't yet understand—behind four simple walls built not just with brick and wood but with hope. Despite the stage you are at on your road to recovery, there is a seat with your name on it, prepared with a feast you won't want to miss.

I moved to North Carolina feeling more lost than found, recovery still so fragile that every gust of fear or loneliness threatened to knock it from my hands. One afternoon, overwhelmed and desperate, I drove aimlessly through unfamiliar streets, searching for something I couldn't name, something that, for a moment, I convinced myself might be found at the bottom of a vodka bottle. I didn't know where I was, but the craving was louder than any logic, so familiar it frightened me. Somewhere between panic and surrender, I pulled my car over, pressed my forehead to the steering wheel, and prayed the simplest prayer I could muster: "God, show me a sign."

When I lifted my head, there it was—a church sign, bold and quiet all at once: Holy Family. The same name of the church where I was raised over four hundred miles away. In that moment, I knew with a certainty that what I needed wasn't a drink, but a door. And God had just opened one. It was especially powerful because when I had entered the dark world of addiction, I had walked away from my faith completely. I had left behind not just the church but any real sense of hope that God still wanted anything to do with someone like me. I had spent years wandering through the wreckage of my own choices, convinced that the distance between me and grace was too wide to ever be crossed. Yet here He was—showing me that the door had never been locked; it was open, waiting for me to find it again. I made a phone call to ask to volunteer. I needed to complete my community service hours, and that day, without fully understanding it, I took the first small step toward rebuilding a life rooted in unity and grace.

But that was only the beginning.

My son's school had a church attached to it. It was a different denomination with different traditions, yet the moment we walked through those doors, we were welcomed without hesitation. They wrapped their arms around me as if we had always belonged to one another. These women, and later the men too, stepped into the quiet, aching spaces of my life, the kind that so often go unnoticed, and they filled them with laughter, prayers, encouragement, and the simple but profound gift of presence.

Through them, I found something I hadn't known how to ask for: deep friendships stitched together with threads of honesty and grace. And through those friendships, I met Connie.

In the beginning, I didn't know how to be friends with women. I was still a stranger to the kind of relationships God had begun weaving into my life. When these women gathered around me—listening patiently, sharing parts of their own journeys, and offering me invitations into their worlds—it felt both beautiful and overwhelming. I wanted more than anything to belong, but years of not-enoughness and awkwardness clung to me like a second skin.

I had built quiet walls around my heart without even realizing it—walls designed to protect me from rejection, disappointment, and getting stuck where I didn't fit. It was easier to hold people at arm's length than to risk being hurt. But love—*real* love, the kind that expects nothing in return—has a way of softening even the most stubborn defenses.

I often say that I am a dip-your-toe-in-the-water kind of person when it comes to relationships. With experiences, I most often dive in headfirst, fearless and reckless. But with people, I inch forward cautiously, clinging to a rope, praying that whatever I'm stepping into won't undo me. That was the only way I knew to move with people most of my life—slowly, carefully, halfway hoping, halfway doubting.

But these women, powerful and patient and full of life, waited with me at the water's edge. They tied their own lines to the shore and offered their life jackets, standing beside me, not pushing or rushing me, just pointing out the beauty floating all around us and warning of the dangers that lurked in the waves of life. They prepared me for the deeper waters of trust, and they celebrated every small step I dared to take further away from the safe shoreline.

God had no intention of letting me stay on that shoreline forever, and neither did they.

Connie especially would not let go; she was persistent. What started as occasional conversations about addiction and recovery soon deepened into a bond marked by both heartbreak and hope. As you read in her letter to the loved ones of the addicted at the beginning of this book, her sister Amanda was fighting her own battle with addiction, and our cautious conversations eventually grew into sacred spaces where grief and hope coexisted.

When Amanda passed away alone in her apartment from an overdose, my heart shattered alongside Connie's. In the heavy silence that grief leaves behind, something remarkable happened: we found each other. And somehow, through pain and prayer, we found unity, too.

Soon after, Connie invited me to contribute to an anthology she was leading through Women World Leaders ministry. I resisted, full of excuses, convinced my life was too busy, too complicated, too fragile to carry one more thing. But God had opened a door, and I had promised to walk through whatever He placed before me. It took courage for her to ask me, and so I answered "yes" with courage.

The first Zoom call unnerved me—women praying out loud with fervor and authority. I had never witnessed faith so raw; it made me feel vulnerable. I sat there, wondering how I had ended up in a place that felt so foreign, certain that I didn't belong. Every part of me wanted to bolt. But I stayed, clinging to my commitment to God rather than my comfort or my commitment to Connie.

I stumbled my way through those calls, through writing deadlines, through the ache of feeling like a misfit among polished voices. When the book launched, I told myself it was a good experience but a one-time thing. I quietly vowed never to do it again.

But God had a different plan. I was invited into a second anthology. And during that year and a half of the same showing up and being obedient, something started to shift. I started looking forward to the meetings. I started taking the things I had heard and learned in those meetings and carried them into my daily life.

After the second anthology, I stood in my kitchen, exhausted yet full of gratitude, telling God once more that I was done, only to feel an immediate vision download into my spirit—a new book, led alongside my friend Connie, called *Faith Unchained: Climbing to Freedom by God's Grace*. It would be filled with stories of women who had broken free from bondage and found freedom through faith.

I couldn't shake it. I couldn't ignore it. I couldn't pretend it was anything but what it was—another call. Another chance to serve in gratitude for my recovery and offer hope the same way the people before me had offered it.

So, I said yes again and once more, the walls crumbled, the friendships deepened, and the connections multiplied. This time, the unity being forged was powerful. It took what was becoming a stagnant connection with my Creator and propelled me to another level of my spiritual path. It opened spaces to encourage other authors to share their testimonies and the world to receive insight for healing. And for me? Well, there were several unexpected blessings, including plenty of room for me to continue learning and growing—some days overwhelmingly so.

Nine years prior, I had just moved to North Carolina. I had been lost in my car, looking for an excuse to relapse. Now, because I stepped into a church full of then strangers and asked for help, dared to say yes to uncomfortable things, and leaned into faith rather than fear, I have built a life stitched together by spiritual connections, books, writing, friendships, and circles of people who show up raw, real, authentic, and ready to love unconditionally.

These people are from different political views, different religious denominations, different backgrounds, and different walks of life. Some share my roots. Some do not. But we are bound by something so deep, something invisible yet undeniably strong—unity.

Unity born from faith is a remarkable collection of invisible threads that wrap themselves tenderly around hearts, moments, and miracles, tying them together into a tapestry far more beautiful than anything we could weave alone. Unity is the synchronicities, divine appointments, and sacred nudges that propel us toward a destiny we cannot always see but can, somehow, still trust.

For most of my life, I believed there would never be a seat for me at any table. As a young girl, I often hid in the bathroom at school during lunch, sitting in a stall with my brown paper bag, because it felt safer to be invisible than to sit alone in plain sight. The walls around me felt protective back then, but they were prison walls, too. Walls that kept me isolated from the belonging my heart desperately needed.

My perception of religion and faith in my early years was completely different than it is today. Recovery has changed the way I see and understand many things. I once thought of religion as rigid, a list of rules and expectations too heavy to carry. I thought faith was something reserved for the perfect, the polished, the ones who never doubted. Today, through connections with people from all walks of life, my worldview has changed dramatically.

Following this path—stepping into the four walls we call the church, recovery groups, homeless shelters, and sex trafficking safe houses—has offered me a different insight. I have friends who show up when surgeries keep me down and friends who gather to worship, discern, and unravel the mysteries of life on life's terms. We grieve together. We celebrate life from its first breath to its final whisper. We walk side by side, bound together by the unity of the Holy Spirit.

Today, not only do I have a seat at the table—I have a seat at *many* tables. If you're reading this and wondering if there's a place for you, too, I want you to know there is. There's a seat saved right next to me, waiting just for you. There are many seats waiting for you next to many people! And if you're still doubting, wondering if you could ever truly belong somewhere, the answer is yes, you absolutely belong.

A quiet kind of courage blooms the moment we dare to walk through unfamiliar doors—the ones framed not just with brick and mortar but with hope. These gathering places I speak of are not just buildings with four walls; they are meeting places where souls searching for something more can experience unity as love and respect stitch strangers into family.

Maybe you have spent years thinking that church—or recovery meetings, or any place, for that matter—wasn't for you. Perhaps you have carried the weight of feeling like an outsider, certain there would be no seat left for someone with a past like yours. But what if I told you your seat has been waiting all along? Even now, somewhere beyond fear and hesitation, a community exists that will not demand perfection but will celebrate your very presence as a gift.

There are no places or people that are perfect. Everywhere we go in this life, we will face imperfect moments. We will be surrounded by imperfect hands and imperfect hearts—just like yours and just like mine. But, if you look closely, you will find invisible threads tying moments together: a shared prayer, a potluck meal after surgery, a hand resting quietly on a grieving shoulder, a voice reading aloud from a Bible once feared to be too heavy to understand. You will find moments of beauty and hope woven between the disappointments.

You don't have to know all the answers to belong. You don't have to have your faith fully figured out to find your way home. You only have to walk into wherever your heart is leading you. Sit. Listen. Be still long enough to hear the heartbeat of unity that has been pulsing there, waiting for you.

Each person you meet will carry wisdom you didn't know you needed. Each story you hear will soften some hidden place inside you that you thought would stay hardened forever. And you, with all your wonderings and imperfections, will carry wisdom they didn't know they were desperate to hear. The exchange will leave you in awe.

Unity begins with a single step. Sometimes awkward, sometimes terrifying, sometimes so small it feels like it could be swallowed by fear. But take that step anyway. Trust that a holy thread will catch you and lead you exactly where you are meant to be.

And one day, you will look around—maybe over coffee in a fellowship hall, maybe during a hymn sung by voices not quite in tune—and realize you are no longer a visitor but part of a living, breathing family bound together by grace that holds a seat at the table for you.

Reflection

Are you still standing on the edges of your own life, wondering if there's a place for you? How often have you held back, waiting for someone to invite you forward? Is it really the lack of invitation that's kept you away... or is it fear that once you sit down, people might see the parts of you you've tried to hide?

What if belonging isn't about finding the perfect table but choosing to show up at the imperfect ones—those with chipped plates, mismatched chairs, and people just as unfinished as you?

Belonging isn't found by waiting. It's discovered when we show up anyway—scars, doubts, and all—believing there's still a place to be seen, heard, and loved. The table has already been set, and your seat is waiting for you to simply show up. This is your invitation.

CHAPTER FIVE

Unity Through Amends: Same Love, New View

"We are not the same persons this year as last; nor are those we love. It is a happy chance if we, changing, continue to love a changed person."
— *W. Somerset Maugham*

L ove doesn't always come wrapped the way we expect. Sometimes, it's only in hindsight that we begin to understand how deeply we were loved or how differently that love was expressed. My relationship with my mom is a perfect example of that. The love between us was always there, but for years, we viewed each other through different lenses.

On the surface, we built a lifetime of beautiful memories: family dinners, shared laughter, holidays, and late-night talks over coffee. There was so much to be grateful for. But beneath it all lived something unspoken. A quiet tension I didn't always have the words for.

From the time I was little, people told me I looked like my Nona—my mom's mother. But it wasn't just my face or the way I moved. I had her fire—her ability to charm, improvise, and make things happen when there was no plan in sight. If we decided to play outside and splash in the water, Nona would head down to her sewing shop and, within what felt like minutes, whip up a bathing suit. She was a war bride who lived on a farm in Naples, Italy, through World War II.

When you come from that kind of experience, you have no choice but to learn to be creative. She could take nothing and turn it into something. She had one of the most visionary minds and a way of putting it to use that left me in complete awe, standing there wide-eyed as I watched her work.

And somewhere along the way, I inherited that same ability.

My mom would get so frustrated when she saw me emulate my grandmother—making something out of nothing and, beyond that, finding every shortcut imaginable and somehow making it work. When my mom seemed displeased with how I was tackling a task, I'd shrug it off and say, "Work smarter, not harder." Without missing a beat, she'd shoot back, "Smart people go to college and get degrees." And I'd just smile and tell her, "I plan to go into real estate sales. I don't need college for that."

That's usually where the conversation ended, but not without lingering tension.

The truth is, I was never a scholastic child, and I don't think either of my parents really believed I was capable of continuing an education beyond high school. And for a long time, I believed that, too.

My mom, on the other hand, had chosen a different path. A righteous one. She valued education deeply and built a respected career in healthcare. She didn't just work within the system—she fought to break barriers for women, pushing her way into management roles at a time when few women held leadership positions. She believed in doing things "the right way"—the clean-cut, safe way. Success, in her eyes, came through discipline, order, and hard work.

And me? I didn't fit that mold.

One of my earliest memories of how differently we saw the world happened one day after Sunday school. I came home beaming with pride, clutching a picture I had colored that morning. I couldn't wait to show her. In my childlike heart, I had imagined her hanging it on the refrigerator, smiling at my creativity.

But the moment she saw it, her expression shifted from curiosity to shock. "Melissa, why on earth did you color Jesus's face purple?" She acted as if I had done something sacrilegious. And in that moment, I was devastated. She didn't wait for an explanation. She was too upset by the "wrong color" to hear anything else.

I remember exactly why I chose that color. That day in class, we learned that purple represented creativity and royalty. And in my little heart, it made perfect sense—Jesus was the King, and He was the most creative in the way He led the apostles. To me, it was the most beautiful, thoughtful choice I could have made. But she never heard that part. And I learned an early, painful lesson that day—sometimes people care more about things "looking right" than understanding the heart behind them.

We clashed often after that—not always with loud explosions but with tension that pulled like a string stretched too far. And now, with years of distance and healing behind me, I wonder if some of that friction had less to do with who I was and more to do with who my mother saw when she looked at me. Maybe it felt like looking into a mirror she wasn't prepared to face—one that reflected her own unresolved memories and silent regrets.

I can't say for sure. But I do know this: the way she looked at me reflected her expectations, worries, and even judgments shaped by the life she had lived. Just as my view of her was shaped by mine.

And isn't that the truth for all of us? We see others as *we* are. Our perception of others is strongly influenced by our own internal state, values, and experiences.

We often forget that our parents aren't just our parents. They are human. With their own hurts and heartbreaks, silent battles, and unmet dreams. I spent years wishing my mom would love me more freely, accept me as I was, and understand that my different way of being wasn't wrong but simply my own. Recovery taught me to see her with a new view. I no longer saw her as the woman who, at times, let me down, but as a woman who did the best she could with what she had. Just like me.

And yet, despite all of our differences, we spent so much time together—me, my mom, and Nona. Three generations of women, beautifully woven together by love, even when tangled in misunderstanding. We traveled, shopped, and spent long afternoons in deep conversations over pastries and coffee. And when I became a mother, that circle grew. I can still picture my babies being cradled in Nona's arms and doted over by my mom. Each of us carried our own stories and way of loving. Perfect or not, those moments mattered.

My mom and I shared experiences that many mothers and daughters only dream of—weekend getaways, deep conversations about life, and the kind of connection every mother hopes to have with her daughter. We planned weddings, hosted birthdays and baby showers, and poured our hearts into every little detail. Those times meant everything to me—a quiet reminder that beneath the tension and misunderstandings, love still flowed steadily between us.

Just as I reflect on the happy memories, the challenging ones surface too. There was a conversation early in my recovery that pierced straight through me. My mom and I were driving to a counseling session when she turned to me and asked, "Why are we going through all this work if you might just drink again?"

I understand now that she wasn't trying to be cruel. She was exhausted by my addiction and, more so, by my relapses. She wanted the nightmare to end, to have her daughter whole again with an absolute black-and-white promise that relapse wasn't possible. That's what I wanted, too. But recovery doesn't follow the timelines we set. It unfolds one slow, painstaking, beautiful day at a time.

In the car that day, I tried to explain the disease of addiction to my mom. I compared it to diabetes, something she understood because she lived with it. But in that moment, she wasn't receptive to the comparison. She was simply a mother who just wanted her child back. And when she couldn't understand, it wasn't because she didn't care—it was because she cared so deeply it terrified her that she couldn't fix my situation for me. The loss of control was an uncomfortable place she spent her entire life trying to avoid. But my addiction had dragged her into that spot, and she was desperate to get away from it.

A few years into my recovery, everything changed. Just as I was making real progress—healing relationships, making amends, and finding steady ground—my mom was diagnosed with Alzheimer's. Nothing prepares you for what that truly means. The woman who had always held everything together, who worked so hard to create a "perfect" world, began slipping away before our eyes. The routines, the control, the roles she clung to for so long—one by one, they fell away, becoming part of a past she could no longer fully grasp.

Alzheimer's is a progressive, degenerative brain disease that slowly erases memory, thinking skills, and, eventually, the ability to perform even the simplest daily tasks. What makes it truly devastating is that as it takes the person's memory from them, it also slowly takes the person who is afflicted from their loved ones, even while they're still living. Family and friends begin to grieve the loss of their loved one long before the body of the Alzheimer's patient gives out. I can tell you that losing my mom to Alzheimer's is like watching her slip through my fingertips. No matter how tightly I try to hold on, I can do nothing to stop her decline and eventual retreat from this world. And even worse, I have witnessed the impact it has on her caretaker—my older and only sister, Adrienne

The grief I've experienced during my mom's illness is oddly familiar—it's the same uneasy, melancholy hopelessness as loving someone lost in addiction. However, there is one stark difference. With addiction, there is hope for a brighter tomorrow. But with Alzheimer's, the days get progressively darker, moving slowly toward an inevitable end—a reality that sits heavy on the heart. Even in acknowledging that difference, as I've watched my mom, I have become better able to understand what she went through as she was losing me down the dark path of addiction.

As my mom's disease progressed, my sister stepped up to care for her full-time, moving back into our childhood home. And I, living states away, felt the crushing weight of guilt and helplessness for not being able to assist her.

My sister and I stay in touch daily, sharing the heartbreak, the exhaustion, and whatever else we need to get off our chests. She fills me in on everything about Mom. She is thankful for the safe space to vent her caregiver woes, and I appreciate learning the details of their daily life that I would otherwise miss if she didn't take the time to communicate. And when they visit me for extended stays, I get the chance to step into that space—to care for my mom, help my sister, and offer love in its most humble form.

One day, during a particularly difficult visit, my mom had an accident in the living room. It was messy—the kind of moment no one talks about, but anyone who's been there knows all too well. Mom didn't make it to the bathroom in time, and, instead, my living room area rug took the job that a toilet normally would. Then my mom walked all through it and circled the open floor plan, leaving footprints of her accident everywhere she had walked. My home's warm, cozy smell was replaced with an odor that nearly peeled paint off the walls. It was a terrible mess.

My sister, exhausted beyond words, excused herself to the bathroom. She didn't say much. She just quietly slipped away and slumped onto the floor between the sink and the toilet, letting the weight of it all crash down as she cried. I assumed the meltdown was the result of many moments like these piling up, but this time I was there to witness it firsthand.

And there I was, standing in the middle of the mess.

In years past, this would have been my breaking point. I had spent so much of my life submitting to my OCD tendencies of keeping everything clean and in perfect order. I would have a clear meltdown if something was out of place or the floor got dirty. I craved control, and that control showed up in the appearance of my environment.

But not this time. This time, something shifted.

I didn't see a disaster; I saw an opportunity. A chance to step in with love instead of frustration. I recognized this was a moment where my sister and I—two daughters who had once made our own childhood messes while our mother cleaned up after us—could now come together in unity to care for the woman who had always been there, cleaning up not just our spills and toys, but also the emotional messes we left in our wake through our adolescence and adulthood.

Tears ran down my face as I began shampooing the carpet—not from frustration, but from a love so deep it broke me wide open. I wasn't angry or overwhelmed by it. I felt honored that I was present and able to step in and help remedy the situation.

This—this was the real work of love and a living amends.

When the house was finally calm, my mom—fresh and cleaned up by my sister—sat quietly on the couch, her cup of tea warming her hands. She looked up at me, and for a moment, the disease of Alzheimer's seemed to push to the side. She recognized me. And in that brief, beautiful moment of clarity, she smiled and said, "Thank you. I love you."

And just like that, after all the years of trying to earn her approval, I finally felt it. Not in grand gestures or perfectly spoken words, but in a look, a smile, and a quiet thank you after a moment of unimaginable vulnerability.

That's what it means to love unconditionally: To meet each other, not with judgment or control, but with presence. To stop trying to shape people into what *we* think they should be and, instead, accept them for who they already are and walk beside them through life.

In recovery, we begin to understand that we have the ability to love one another—fully, freely, and without the need for perfection. Recovery didn't just change me; it changed how I love.

As my mom's memory fades, mine grows sharper. Not with resentment but with gratitude.

And now, standing on the other side of that relationship, I try to parent my own children differently. I'm intentional about it. I tell myself I won't repeat the patterns. I won't let my need for control drown out their voices or their dreams. I want them to know they are loved exactly as they are—not as who I hope they'll become someday. It is my desire to be their safe place. Their sounding board.

Those attempts are just some of my living amends to them.

But even as I work so hard to break those generational cycles, I can almost see them keeping a mental list of all the ways they'll do it differently when they become parents.

Because the truth is, no matter how hard we try, we'll always leave something behind for the next generation to wrestle with. And maybe that's okay. Because life isn't about being perfect.

Learning to live in recovery includes embracing our imperfections with humility and grace. It is stepping out to love others and allowing ourselves to be loved. It is about leading by example, even when that example is admitting we don't always get it right.

Despite all the ways I try to get it right, I still fall short. I still miss moments. And that's where the real work begins—in the repair. In the quiet amends we make, not with grand gestures, but with simple, honest conversations that begin with, "I'm sorry. I'm learning, too."

One day, when my mom takes her final breath and no longer has to battle the terrible disease of Alzheimer's, my love for her will remain eternal, and my gratitude will run deep. When she is gone, it will be the same love—but a different view. And as I grow older and one day look to my own children to help me through my elder years, I pray their love for me will surpass any of my shortcomings as a mother—that their love, too, will be the same, but a beautifully different view.

Reflection

In the chaos of real life—in the wiping of tears, the scrubbing of floors, the quiet offering of presence—we discover the truest form of amends. It's not about having all the answers. There's no perfect manual for living—for parenting, being a daughter or son or friend, or getting everything right. But there is this: a willingness to show up, stay present, and love through the messy, imperfect, and difficult moments.

So, pause and ask yourself: Where do I need to loosen control, show up more fully, and love someone exactly as they are today? You might just find that's where the deepest joy of unity begins.

Love isn't found just in the easy moments; it's forged in the humbling spaces where we choose each other over and over again.

CHAPTER SIX

The Disconnect in People-Pleasing

*I can't give you a sure-fire formula for success, but I can give you a
formula for failure: try to please everybody all the time."*
—Herbert Bayard Swope

For most of my life, I thought people-pleasing was one of
my better qualities, until I learned that it is an unhealthy
attempt at unity that can be disguised as love. On the surface,
people-pleasing looks like kindness—saying yes, showing up,
pushing ourselves to meet everyone's expectations. In my efforts
to please others, I even took pride in my Martha Stewart-inspired
Christmases, crafting every detail to perfection. People would
look at the events I pulled off—the decorations, the food, the
atmosphere—and say, "You're the party planner of the year! You
should do this for a living!" And I'd smile, but inside, I was
screaming, *Are you kidding me? I don't even enjoy this!*

But when someone asked me to do something, I stepped up and
gave it one hundred percent—not because I loved it, but because
I was chasing something. I wasn't striving to be the best; I was
desperate for validation. *Melissa's good at something. Melissa's good*

at this or that. Those praises became my lifeline, even though they came at a cost. And the unfortunate part was that no matter how many compliments I collected, they never filled my voids.

In active addiction, my need for validation only grew louder. I couldn't keep my commitments or show up for the people I loved, and every time I failed, I buried myself a little deeper under the weight of guilt and shame. My life didn't revolve around keeping promises—it revolved around keeping my addiction alive. And the harder I tried to prove that I was dependable, the more painfully obvious it became that I wasn't.

At first glance, it might have looked like I was the ultimate giver, always saying yes and always showing up. But the reality was far more complicated. I wasn't saying yes out of joy or a genuine desire to help—I was saying yes because I couldn't bear the thought of being seen as anything less than needed, helpful, or essential. That's the part of people-pleasing no one wants to admit. It looks like selflessness, but often, it's a hidden search for approval dressed up as acts of good deeds.

In recovery, I've had to face this hard truth. What I once called "service" was often a transaction. I gave my time and energy, hoping deep down to fill the emptiness inside me—the aching belief that I wasn't enough unless I was doing something for someone else and earning their seal of approval.

Before recovery, I didn't have boundaries at all. I lived in a constant state of overextension or complete withdrawal—either giving everything I had until I collapsed or isolating when the weight of unmet commitments became too heavy to bear. I didn't know how to balance life—probably because I was too busy spinning my wheels between a bottle of vodka and a secret stash of pills while just barely getting by in between. I didn't know how to live balanced or healthy in any aspect of my life. I desperately wanted to, but I had no clue how to get there. And because I had spent so many years saying yes to everything and everyone, the people around me naturally came to expect that version of me.

But when I entered recovery, I started learning a different way. I began to understand that boundaries weren't walls to keep people out—they were fences with gates, and I had the power to operate their open and closed positions. This new understanding allowed me to show up for others without losing myself in the process. As I slowly started incorporating boundaries, something became painfully clear: the people I loved didn't quite know what to do with this new version of Melissa.

The real turning point came when I realized how exhausted, resentful, and empty I felt after constantly overextending myself. Once the veil of drugs and alcohol was lifted, I could see things from a different viewpoint. I recognized I wasn't saying yes out of joy or generosity; I was saying yes because I didn't know how to say no. And when I did try to set limits, the discomfort felt unbearable and sometimes even tense. People had grown used to me being the person who always said yes, who bent and broke herself to meet every need. And now, all of a sudden, I was showing up differently—with limits. Saying no. Speaking up when something didn't sit right with me. And for those who had benefited from my lack of boundaries for years, this shift felt like rejection or selfishness.

But I wasn't trying to push anyone away. It was about finally honoring the space I needed to heal, grow, and stay well. And while it was hard for others to adjust, it was even harder for me to stand firm when their discomfort surfaced. Yet, that's where the real growth happened—right in the middle of that tension.

I wanted to be acknowledged, respected, and understood. But the way I delivered that message didn't come out easily or land where it needed to. I wasn't able to simply exercise my new voice; it was more like an exorcism. I physically had to push my feelings out of my body, which came in the form of blurting out and yelling. It was awkward and, quite frankly, sometimes downright embarrassing.

I'd swallowed my feelings and pushed aside my needs for so long that when I finally tried to release them, I felt I had to force the words—as if the only way they could escape was by being shouted out. I didn't calmly express my boundaries or needs; I announced them forcefully. I'd go from total silence to explosive declarations like, "I have a voice in this situation!" or "I have the right to be heard!" I cried out, like a child who's been ignored for too long, desperate for someone to see and hear me.

My middle child syndrome shot straight to the surface like a life preserver held underwater and then suddenly released—propelling itself high above the surface, bursting through the air of vulnerability, and then simply bobbing there, exposed and unsteady, floating awkwardly in plain view.

My attempts didn't invite healthy conversation or mutual understanding, but instead, startled people and shut them down. And in those moments, the very connection I longed for moved further out of reach.

And because I would lash out in those ways—exploding when my boiling point was finally crossed—nothing ever truly got resolved. Once I hit that limit, whatever the other person had done, whatever part they played in the situation was instantly overshadowed by my reaction. The focus shifted entirely onto my outburst and my emotional unraveling.

In that instant, any opportunity for growth vanished. There was no light shed on their part in the dysfunction, no room for them to reflect or take responsibility. And there was certainly no growth on my end because all the attention was locked onto the behavior I had created—the meltdown I had delivered.

It became a cycle of self-sabotage. At the end of each cycle, I would tell myself, *I am never speaking up again, just so at the end of it all, I have to eat my own words and not be heard. This is impossible!*

But even those clumsy messy moments mattered. Because every time I tried, I got a little closer to figuring it out. I learned how to take a breath before I spoke. I began to trust that my voice did matter, although it needed to come out a little softer and steadier. And, over time, I discovered I didn't have to scream to be heard—I just had to believe that I was worthy of being listened to and find a way to get my point across that didn't invalidate the feelings of the person I was trying to communicate with.

I'm still working on this. Even as I sit here writing this chapter, a situation recently came up where I felt so certain about something, so convicted in my stance, that I charged forward full steam ahead. But in my certainty, I failed to slow down and communicate clearly. I didn't consider the people around me. I didn't respect their boundaries or give space for their voices.

Once I recognized my actions, they hit me hard. I knew I had to acknowledge the situation and put a full stop to it, which I did: "I see it clearly now. I bulldozed ahead. This is one of the things I still struggle with. It wasn't fair to you. That was never my intention, but I understand now how it landed—and it wasn't right. Can we take a step back and try again? This time, I'll really listen, and I hope you'll also hear where I'm coming from. Let's work toward a decision that feels right for both of us."

That was the outcome this time. But believe me, I didn't get from one year of sobriety—still raw, attending treatment centers, and sitting in DUI accountability courts—to that kind of healthy, mature resolution overnight. It took years of practice. Years of falling flat on my face, of getting it wrong before I started getting it right. Like physical exercise, you don't build strength with a couple of sit-ups and expect to win a weightlifting competition. You have to put in the work every single day and choose progress over perfection through each step of growth.

That's how it is with finding your voice, learning discernment, and practicing communication and healthy confrontation. You don't wake up one day magically knowing how to do it all. Let's cut ourselves some slack here and give ourselves some grace for a change. We learn through practice and gain through losses. As we strive to accomplish, we strengthen our faith in ourselves and our Higher Power through prayer, reflection, and showing up imperfectly to try again.

And let me share with you the best part...

Most of the time, now I can go to others with calm, level-headedness, and respect and say, "You know what? I didn't handle that the right way. I was trying to make you happy," or "I wanted to do the best job at this," or "I thought I was doing what was right,"—whatever the truth is in that moment. Then, I follow it with the most important part: "But I didn't consider your feelings, and I recognize that this is a pattern I'm still working through. I'm grateful for your patience as I continue to grow. I want to be a better friend," "A better co-worker," "A better spouse," or "A better mother for you." And then I tell the person, with all sincerity, "How you feel matters, too."

More often than not, that vulnerability opens the door to grace. People aren't usually looking for perfection—they're looking for humility and sincerity. They want someone who is willing to admit when they get it wrong and is committed enough to keep working as they seek to make amends and commit to positive change.

That's the kind of freedom recovery offers us—not the freedom to do it perfectly, but the freedom to do it differently. Every time we choose humility over pride, connection over control, and honesty over avoidance, we take one more step toward becoming the people we are intended to be through divine design.

Be aware that when we've had that breakthrough—when we finally understand why we've lived in the exhausting cycle of people-pleasing and that it no longer serves us or the people we love—it's natural to start expecting those around us to understand where we are and the process we've gone through. Always remember: just because you've had a moment of clarity doesn't mean everyone else has arrived at that same place.

Always walk forward from each breakthrough with an attitude of grace, understanding that not everyone has had your experience or come to the same understanding you have. And isn't it beautiful to know that you don't have to demand it of them? Instead, you get to share your growth and experience with others in a way that will empower them without dismissing or diminishing where they are in their own journey.

Setting boundaries to step out of people-pleasing requires us to love and respect ourselves as much as we love and respect others. And while loving others unconditionally supports recovery, sometimes, unconditional love looks like knowing better for yourself while not expecting someone on the other side of your experience to know the same thing. Unconditional love is more than being able to meet someone where they are; it's also loving someone where they are while continuing to stand firmly in the truth you've worked so hard to discover for yourself.

This meet-in-the-middle communication we have been discussing—the daily, intentional work of showing up honestly, openly, and humbly—leads to unity and connections deeper than we could have ever understood in active addiction. Fruitful, beautiful, meaningful relationships are waiting for us, and the truth is, we are worthy of them. Just as important, other people are worthy of receiving love from us that lifts them up rather than weighs them down.

That's the kind of connection we're talking about here—the kind where we show up as unique human beings, each designed differently, working together in this world with honesty and grace. When we meet each other right where we are, telling the truth about who we are and finding acceptance in that sacred space, we create a connection that doesn't just change *our* lives—it changes the world. This is the baseline of love we're called to offer one another. And quite frankly, it's the same love we must finally learn to give ourselves. The freedom that comes when we are able to share unconditional love with others and ourselves is extraordinary. Once you begin to tap into it and experience it, it's hard to live life any other way. Unconditional love can fill our voids in a way that people-pleasing never can.

I might be on a never-ending search for the balance between pleasing God, pleasing myself, and pleasing others. But I know for certain that the journey itself and the discovery along the way deliver the most profound and miraculous moments. I also know that when the hard work is done, some of the greatest joy in this life will be found. What can be more pleasing than that?

Reflection

If you're trapped in the exhausting cycle of people-pleasing—saying yes when you mean no or silencing your voice until it explodes from you—pause now and take a deep breath. You don't have to have it all figured out today. Ask yourself gently: What is my part in this? Where can I grow? How can I respond differently next time? Journal about it. Lean on your Higher Power for direction.

And when the time comes, don't be afraid to use your voice—even if it shakes. You might be surprised how often a simple, heartfelt "I'm still working on this, and I'm grateful for your patience" is all it takes to invite grace into the conversation.

When you say yes authentically, it will no longer be a silent cry for validation—it will be a true, joy-filled offering of your whole, healthy heart.

CHAPTER SEVEN

Thank You for Your Service

"United we stand, divided we fall."
—John Dickinson

W hen I first began my recovery journey, the thought of venturing beyond the familiar rooms of 12-step meetings and counseling sessions felt overwhelming. Those rooms were safe—filled with people who spoke my language and understood the weight I carried and the daily battles I fought. But there comes a time in recovery when the walls that protect us begin to confine us. Eventually, we become brave and strong enough to look for open doors instead of protective walls.

Recovery isn't about building a fortress to keep life out. It's about creating a foundation sturdy enough to help us remain steady as we step back into the world—one experience, one relationship, one adventure at a time. One of those adventures should include seeking to serve others. We discussed service in Chapter Three, but as you grow and your circle of influence widens, it's crucial to maintain a humble, servant attitude. Your ongoing willingness to step out and share your time and energy can take you places you never thought of and bring you shoulder-to-shoulder with people you never imagined meeting.

In my willingness to serve, I recently had the honor of participating in the Triad Honor Flight, a journey from North Carolina to Washington, D.C., designed to celebrate and honor our nation's veterans. I wasn't just a passenger on this flight—I had the privilege of serving as a guardian, walking alongside these incredible men and women as they revisited the monuments and memorials that tell the story of their sacrifices.

I was there for my dear friend, Tina—a retired commander in the U.S. Navy, a woman who broke barriers and built a legacy long before I ever found the courage to break free from my own chains of addiction.

Tina and I met in a way that could only be described as divine timing. When I first arrived at Holy Family, the church where I now work and serve, I was a bundle of nerves. New environments still made me uneasy. Though I was learning to trust again, my walls were firmly intact. Tina recognized the fear behind my walls and met me with grace, not judgment.

She greeted me often with a warmth that felt like sunshine cutting through a foggy morning. She didn't push or prod but simply kept showing up. Week after week, she offered her smile, prayers, and gentle encouragement. She believed in me before I learned to believe in myself. Somewhere along the way, our friendship began to form—a bond built on quiet persistence and genuine care.

When Tina asked me to accompany her on this Honor Flight, I felt the weight of what she was really asking. She wasn't just inviting me on a trip. She was trusting me to walk alongside her on a sacred journey filled with memories of her own sacrifice and service.

Although I had gotten to know Tina over the years on a spiritual level, the two of us had never spent time together alone outside the walls of the church. And I'll admit—I was intimidated going into this event. *Would I be good enough? Would I live up to the expectations of the role of a guardian?* As we traveled together, sharing about our life circumstances and getting to know each other more deeply, a quiet fear crept in—*Would she decide I wasn't a good enough friend?*

Even after all my time in recovery, making new friends isn't always easy. Putting myself out there and stepping into unfamiliar situations is still uncomfortable. But as the day went on and Tina and I shared stories back and forth, something beautiful happened. We discovered we had so many things in common, and so many other things in our lives seemed to complement each other perfectly.

The intimate conversations we squeezed in during the flight and on our bus rides between monuments gave me a new appreciation—not only for my dear friend but for the countless sacrifices the men and women of our armed forces have made so that we might live in freedom. More clearly than ever, I also saw the sacrifices other women from generations before me endured to pave the way for the rights, employment options, and countless other opportunities built on equality and safety that we enjoy today.

We boarded that plane surrounded by history itself. Twelve Purple Heart recipients shared that flight with us—four were World War II veterans. I sat beside a man who had lost his leg in Afghanistan, a living testament to the cost of freedom. Although he was a Purple Heart recipient, he was not there as a distinguished guest but to humbly serve as a guardian for another veteran who bore the same honor.

The air on that plane felt different. It wasn't just the hum of engines or the typical buzz of travel but was heavy with stories of loss and triumph and memories too sacred for words. The heaviness was also mixed with celebration. Blue stars adorned the aisle, and an American flag graced the back of each seat. Patriotic music played softly in the background, familiar melodies that seemed to wrap around every heart in the cabin.

As people filtered in to find their assigned seats, I noticed something remarkable. Each honoree carried a light-hearted smile, showcasing their gratitude for the moment at hand. But their eyes held a deeper story. A quiet weight rested behind those eyes, the kind that comes from having lived through things most of us could never fully understand. Many of these people were Vietnam veterans—soldiers who had returned home from their war without the recognition they deserved. They hadn't been greeted with parades or applause; they had returned to silence, and sometimes even hostility. But that day, on that flight, it was different. It was their day to be honored for their sacrifice. It was a moment for their stories to be seen, their service acknowledged, and their courage celebrated.

Throughout the day in Washington, we visited memorial after memorial. Each stone etched with names became a mirror reflecting lives lived with courage. I stood before the World War II Memorial and thought about how, in my own life, I had fought a war that left invisible scars. Addiction may not have made the history books, but it wrote its chapters on my body and soul just the same. And there, among these heroes, I felt something familiar—an unspoken understanding that survival comes at a cost, but it also comes with a purpose.

As we moved from site to site, I found myself asking the veterans a simple question: "What's been your favorite part of the trip so far?" I expected a variety of answers—perhaps a specific memorial or a quiet moment of reflection—but to my surprise, every single veteran echoed the same response. Their favorite part was entering each memorial and being greeted by groups of young people standing proudly with signs and flags, saluting them as they walked by.

Their faces lit up as they spoke of it. This simple yet powerful gesture gave them something more than gratitude—it gave them hope. Hope that the next generation understands their sacrifices and holds a deep respect for what it takes to secure and preserve freedom. That moment—seeing young hearts honoring old heroes—felt like a passing of the torch, a living reminder that the courage of these brave veterans had not been forgotten and their sacrifices would live on in the hearts of those who follow.

Yet even as their faces lit up in those moments of honor, I couldn't help but think about the struggles many of our veterans continue to carry quietly after all the ceremonies end and the crowds go home. Their world was rocked by warfare. It began with deployment and was marked by long stretches of time spent away from their families. They saw unspeakable things and witnessed and endured hardships that most of us can't begin to imagine. Yet, when they returned home, carrying memories and images that refused to fade, they were expected to reintegrate into a life that, for many, felt foreign.

Too often, these heroes returned, not to a warm embrace but to a world that felt indifferent or even unkind. Some never received the support and infrastructure needed to heal from their experiences. Some still walk through life every day with their emotions pinned tightly inside and their memories sealed away because the weight feels too heavy to share.

Many veterans struggle with severe Post Traumatic Stress Disorder (PTSD) and mental health issues. Some turn to substances or alcohol to numb the pain. These are the unseen consequences of their sacrifice—wounds that don't always bleed outwardly but cut just as deep.

It's not enough for us to honor them with words alone. We must be willing to support them with our actions—to offer an ear, lend a hand, or help however we can. We are called to show up, listen with compassion, and demonstrate with our lives that we are truly proud, honored, and grateful for the freedoms so many fought to protect. The freedoms we enjoy were earned at a great cost—and it's our duty to ensure that those who paid the price are never forgotten or left behind.

I was never in the military, but having the honor of serving our veterans that day stirred something deep inside me, bringing back memories from my childhood. I remember curling up in my grandfather's lap, begging him to tell me stories of his service in World War II with the U.S. Army, including how he met my grandmother while stationed in Italy. I also loved listening to her version—how she became a war bride and what it was like to have the military enter their village, take over their family farms, and set up defense in the caves that once held their wine and dry goods. Every time my grandfather told his stories, I would catch a new detail, something I hadn't heard before, and cling to it, asking him more and more questions.

Those stories were my first lessons about sacrifice, bravery, and the complicated cost of freedom. And there I was, decades later, walking among the living reminders of those same lessons.

At the Vietnam Veterans Memorial, I saw Tina pause. Her fingers traced the cold black granite, lingering over names that surely stirred memories. I didn't ask. Some moments are too sacred for words. Instead, I stood quietly beside her, humbled by the honor of simply being there.

That day didn't just shift my perspective—it confirmed my calling. For years, I wrestled with whether I should recover out loud. There's a safety in anonymity, a comfort in keeping the mess of your past tucked away behind closed doors. But walking beside those men and women—people who had made themselves vulnerable by literally putting their lives on the line for others—reminded me that bravery isn't just found on battlefields. Bravery is found every time we choose to step into the light and say, "This is my story."

The sacrifices of our veterans paved the way for freedom, not only for their own generation but for every generation that would follow. And isn't that what I'm called to do as well? To stand in the light of my recovery, share the unpleasant parts, and hold up a lantern of hope so those still lost in the dark can find their way?

That day, I felt a profound understanding settle deep within my soul. The freedoms I have today—to recover from substance use disorder, to access healthcare for my mental health, to stand on public platforms and recover out loud, to write this very book and express every raw, honest piece of my journey—are all connected to the brave fights that were fought and won long before me. Every freedom I walk in today is built on the courage and sacrifice of others.

That awareness lit a fire in me that continues to burn. It reminds me that my recovery, finding my voice, and gaining the willingness to share hope are not just personal victories. They are responsibilities. Sacred opportunities to honor the freedom I've been given by using it to lift someone else out of darkness.

As we made our way back home that evening, something inside me shifted. I thought about all the times I had stayed small because I was afraid to fail, be uncomfortable, or try something new. But on that trip, I sat beside men and women who had faced fear head-on. Who had run toward danger so others could live in freedom. And here I was, standing in that freedom—no longer imprisoned by addiction, no longer bound by the belief that my life had to remain small to stay safe.

That flight wasn't just a journey to Washington, D.C. It was a flight into a new understanding of what it means to live free. As I looked around at the veterans and guardians—my new friends gathered together, each with their own story of struggle and triumph—I realized that freedom is not something we're meant to carry alone. It's something we uphold together, side by side. United we stand—not only as a nation but as people committed to lifting one another out of darkness and into the light, one day at a time.

Reflection

There's a moment in every journey when the road ahead looks uncertain, and the familiar comfort of the old life calls you back. But what if the real blessing lies just beyond what feels safe?

For years, I stayed within the walls that made me feel secure. And while there's a time and place for those safe spaces, true healing happens when we dare to step outside them. Some of my greatest blessings have come from saying yes to things that once scared me. New experiences and meeting people who have lived entirely different lives have helped me realize that the world is full of stories waiting to be shared.

Being a part of the Triad Honor Flight confirmed what I've come to understand deep in my soul: We aren't meant to hide the dark parts of our story. We're meant to stand in the light and share them boldly. When we do, we help break the silence for others still suffering in the shadows. And in doing so, we can create new connections, spark hope, and offer a roadmap for freedom.

So I ask you: Where are your walls? And more importantly, how might you take the opportunity to go beyond them? Maybe it's time to sit beside someone whose story is different from yours. To try something that feels a little uncomfortable. To venture out and let life surprise you.

We're not meant to walk this journey alone. The unity we long for often finds us when we least expect it—on flights we almost don't take, in friendships we don't see coming, and in moments when we choose courage over comfort.

Let that truth settle in your heart today. And the next time you feel the pull to stay small, remember—you were made for more. Recovery offers a new world for you to discover.

Timing Is Everything

"Eventually all pieces fall into place... until then, laugh at the confusion, live for the moments, and know everything happens for a reason."
—*Albert Schweitzer*

I have always had a complicated relationship with time. No matter how determined I am to stay ahead of it, time seems to slip through my hands like sand. People who know me know this about me. It's one of those quiet, lingering struggles I've carried for as long as I can remember and is not something I hide, but certainly not something I'm proud of either.

While it might seem like a small thing to some, this ongoing battle with time has become one of my greatest teachers—showing me lessons about patience, humility, integrity, and how life has a way of unfolding exactly when it is meant to, not a moment sooner.

As we recover, we must be attentive to time—honoring schedules for the sake of others and ourselves, appreciating the value of a well-timed pause, and trusting the process of time itself as we grow and become all we are meant to be.

One of my good friends used to tease me about my ongoing struggle with time. Back in my hometown, there was a television network called Turner Broadcasting Station—TBS for short. They had this quirky habit of starting their shows five minutes after the hour. While everyone else began their programs at 7:00 sharp, TBS shows would roll in fashionably late at 7:05. That offbeat timing became their signature—and somewhere along the way, it became mine, too. Every time I'd walk into work running behind, my friend would laugh and say, "There's Melissa. She's on TBS time—always five minutes late."

It was a lighthearted joke, but underneath it, I knew there was a deeper truth I needed to confront. Because here's what I've learned—when we show up late, it's not just about a clock. It's about keeping our word. It's about respect. It's about the kind of life we're building. And for me, every time I showed up late, I wasn't just running behind on the schedule—I was falling behind in the life I promised myself I wanted to live.

For years, I told myself it wasn't a big deal. I worked better under pressure. I was creative in the chaos. But deep down, I knew the truth. As I constantly scrambled and apologized, I felt like I was one step behind—because I was.

And here's the most brutal truth of all: When you don't show up on time, it sends a message. It quietly tells people that their time isn't as valuable as yours. In recovery, where trust is hard-earned and easily broken, that's a message I didn't want to keep sending.

Recovery forced me to be honest with myself. I began to recognize that being punctual is not just about arriving somewhere on time—it's about showing integrity, creating trust, and earning respect.

Honoring time also involves learning to believe that life unfolds exactly as it should if we're patient enough to let it.

I can't tell you how often I've begged for things to happen faster. I wanted broken relationships healed immediately. I willed the cravings to disappear instantly. I desired the restored life I dreamed of to become a reality right away—please and thank you. Sitting in discomfort felt unbearable. Waiting felt like punishment.

But real healing doesn't happen overnight. And the kind of growth that lasts doesn't show up on demand.

For those of us who have lived through addiction, the mindset of instant gratification is second nature. We're conditioned to chase quick relief, fast highs, immediate comfort—whatever it takes to numb the pain. Waiting feels foreign. Sitting with discomfort feels unbearable. And for me, breaking free from that mindset was one of the hardest parts of recovery.

I wanted everything to happen *now*. But recovery doesn't work like that. Life doesn't work like that. And the more I tried to force it, the more frustrated and discouraged I became.

It took time—long, necessary time—to learn that the most valuable things in life don't arrive instantly. They are built slowly, with care, through experience, humility, and grace. And sometimes, the act of waiting—choosing to sit still and stay present in the discomfort instead of reaching for a quick escape—is the very thing that heals us.

Through the unity I found in recovery, I began understanding the necessity of releasing my desperate need for immediate results. I watched others who had walked this path before me and saw a peace in them that wasn't born from an easy life but from learning to pause. They had discovered how to sit with the heavy moments and invite prayer, meditation, and discernment into their decision-making.

As I followed their lead, I began to comprehend the power of the pause—one of the most valuable tools I've used in my long-term sobriety. Pausing includes stopping before reacting, praying before deciding, and listening carefully in an effort to recognize the difference between our ego's voice and our Higher Power's voice.

Over time and with practice, pausing became a habit. And that habit became freedom. Regularly taking a moment of quiet reflection allowed me to move forward, not out of fear or impulse, but from a place of peace and clarity. It taught me how to wait with purpose and trust the timing, believing that if I did the next right thing, my future would unfold as it was meant to.

Pausing is not just a helpful tool for personal recovery; it is also a tool we can use as we walk in unity with someone who needs us. Being there for a loved one often involves pausing and trusting *their* timing.

As a sober, present mom, I now have the privilege and honor of watching my children live this out in their own lives. Each of them—whether they've touched on the depths of what I have through addiction or are simply living out their own life experiences—is living by their timeline. As their mother, I want so badly to pull out all the answers, to lay the map in front of them and smooth the path. But that's not my job.

My job is to walk with them. To stand with them through their losses and cheer them on through their victories. To allow them to make their own decisions and walk their own timelines. That realization has created a new kind of unity within our family—a space where mistakes are allowed, growth is honored, and love is constant.

For those reading this who are the loved ones of people struggling with substance use disorder, this is a profound and deeply challenging process to consider. We have an innate desire to fix problems for those we love—especially for our children, siblings, and closest friends.

And yet, the greatest gift we can offer those we love is not to remedy their problems or do their work for them—it's to create a bubble of unity with them, letting them know, "I see you. You are in a hard place. I don't have all the answers, but I'm here to help you stand and take your next step."

As we pause, we can shower our loved ones with prayer. We can share our perspective. We can help them find support networks that feel good and right for them. And as they walk through their difficult places, we can promise, "I'll be right there with you."

Life often doesn't look perfect. None of us will get it right every time. But we can stand in hope and say, "I know you will find your way because I believe in you."

We can set healthy boundaries that allow us to respect ourselves while showing those we love that we haven't turned our backs on them by letting them know we are patiently waiting for when they are ready to make healthy choices for themselves. Boundaries don't just bring *you* peace; in the long run, they show your loved ones an example of self-love and self-respect. Though your loved one may not be equipped to understand your example until they surrender their addiction, eventually, when they start taking the first steps, they will recognize the seeds you planted for what boundaries should look like. Those seeds may, in time, help them edit their road map.

And here's the beautiful part—as we walk beside our loved ones, willing and available to assist them, we will learn just as much as they will on their own journey. It's a beautiful exchange.

The hardest part about loving an addict is that we can not set a time limit on how long they will be in active addiction. They have to choose to change on their own. And the time we wait for that miracle moment can feel like an eternity.

I want to share a moment in my own recovery and writing journey. This is a moment that helped me understand how things work out over time—not when *we* say, but when the universe lines up and everything falls into perfect order. Not because we've rushed it, but because we find ourselves exactly where we are supposed to be at the exact moment we are supposed to be there.

I had been stalling to write this book for over a year. I took on other writing projects and convinced myself I needed to be more present in different areas of my life. And while there was some truth to that, if I'm completely transparent, I'd spread myself thin after the success of my first book and the birth of my non-profit.

The book opened doors I never imagined. It allowed me to attend in-person meetings and hand out tens of thousands of free copies. But even as I stood in those beautiful moments of connection, I couldn't shake the quiet voice that echoed in my mind almost every day: It's time for the second book.

And sometimes, I would answer back—out loud, "I'm not ready. I don't have it in me." Then fear crept in. *What if this second book doesn't measure up? What if it isn't as successful or as well-received as the first one?* That kind of self-talk is dangerous. And it sat heavy on my heart longer than I want to admit.

The truth is, those thoughts had nothing to do with my calling and everything to do with my ego. My calling is about others. It's about sharing hope, not about protecting my pride.

The call to get this book out started pulsing stronger. The thoughts came more often, like a heartbeat quickening as the body starts to move. But even then, I didn't know where to begin. A heavy blanket of imposter syndrome settled over me, and my creativity flatlined.

Then, one night, I attended a local dinner called Partners in Hope, an event where people gather to raise money for those trying to find solid ground again. Honestly, I didn't want to go. I was exhausted. I had worked all day, and the thought of one more commitment felt like too much. But something in me knew I needed to show up.

As I was leaving, a man approached me. He was standing beside a woman and holding a baby in his arms.

"Do you remember me?" he asked. "I've been meaning to talk to you... and thank you."

In that moment, I saw him clearly. It was John—a friend I'd made along the way. A man who had once walked into the church where I worked, broken and searching for hope. He'd been living out of his car, unemployed, battling depression. I offered him my book, and we spent time talking over several weeks. I didn't tell him what he should do or how he should do it. I didn't try to fix his life for him. I just sat with him and shared experience, strength, and hope. Eventually, he stopped checking in, and I wondered how he was doing. As a matter of fact, he had crossed my mind out of the blue just the day before the dinner.

Suddenly, there he stood—married, a manager at his job, holding his newborn child, smiling, at peace, and full of gratitude. He had found his way through a very long, difficult situation.

As I drove home that night through the dark roads of Winston-Salem, tears filled my eyes and flowed down my cheeks. I cried in awe of the privilege of witnessing someone come through to the other side. And in that quiet moment alone in my car, I knew—without a shadow of a doubt—that this was the stamp on my timeline.

The day had come. It was time to write this book and share how essential unity is in recovery.

It is humbling to acknowledge that each time we answer the call to share hope, we may never fully see the outcome. But that night, I was given a glimpse. In response, I did what we are all asked to do in recovery—I pushed my ego and self-doubt aside and held myself accountable.

I made a phone call to my publisher that very night. By the next day, we were hammering out contracts and setting deadlines. And what happened next was nothing short of extraordinary. The pieces lined up. The impossible became possible. That's the beauty of perfect timing.

That's the beauty of showing up when it's time.

Isn't that what this new life asks of us? To show up. To step forward when that quiet voice starts to stir. To trust that even if we can't see the whole path ahead, the next step will appear when we're ready.

Sometimes, life calls for immediate action. And sometimes, it calls for patience and discernment.

Some things simply need time to unfold. Situations have to play out. Lessons must be lived before we can fully step into the timeline waiting for us.

This much I know for certain—every effort I make to humbly serve and show up for my recovery happens in perfect timing as long as I'm following a will greater than my own...as long as I'm walking forward not driven by ego but by purpose...and as long as I'm willing to take this journey one day at a time, in God's perfect timing.

Reflection

Take a quiet moment and ask yourself: What season am I standing in right now? Am I pushing for something that isn't ready to unfold? Or holding back from a door that's already open?

Wherever you are, trust that you're exactly where you need to be. Waiting doesn't mean you're falling behind. It simply means something is still being prepared—within you and around you.

Keep showing up. Keep listening for that quiet nudge. And when the time is right, you'll know. One day at a time—that's more than enough.

CHAPTER NINE

The 5 Love Languages in Recovery

"Love is a choice you make every day."
—Gary Chapman

When I started writing, I had no idea how far the journey would take me. I just knew that God had pulled me out of addiction for a reason—and that reason was to help someone else find their way home. Early in my journey, God aligned me with someone who would become one of the most powerful influences on my writing and my life: Dr. Gary Chapman, *New York Times* bestselling author of *The 5 Love Languages*, who taught me that there are tools to help us love others better.

Dr. Chapman and I were unlikely friends—me, a woman in recovery with a trail of mug shots and brokenness behind me; him, a highly educated marriage counselor, retired pastor, and worldwide bestselling author who has written over 80 books. But there we were, sitting across from each other in his office, bound together by two powerful forces: God and love.

Dr. Chapman read the raw manuscript of my first book, *I'm Sober... So Now What?: A Journey of Hope and Healing*, before it had any polish or direction. He didn't turn away when this mess of a woman reached out for advice on writing and spiritual direction. Instead, he leaned in. He encouraged me, prayed with me, and walked with me through 152 rejections from agents and publishers. He never let me quit. He told me, "Build your platform, stay connected—and no matter what, don't ever stop writing." He saw something in me. And more than that—he believed in my mission to share hope.

I told Dr. Chapman how his book changed my marriage, but beyond that, it changed the way I related to people in recovery. I also revealed to him how, as I walked this journey, I started to see something powerful: *The 5 Love Languages* aren't just for romantic relationships; they're also essential in healing from addiction. Because recovery is about connection, and love is what holds connection together.

Maybe you're reading this, thinking: *That sounds good, but I don't know how to love. I don't know how to give it or receive it.*

I understand that thought process. That was mine, too. So, let me pause here and speak directly to these concerns.

How can we give love or receive love when years of addiction, trauma, and poor choices have jaded or clouded our reality? How do we embrace connection when isolation has been our normal? When the only version of love we've known came with strings attached—or left us shattered?

Here's the truth: For most of us, addiction wasn't the beginning of our pain—it was a response to it. And when you've spent years numbing, hiding, running, and surviving, the idea of letting someone in—of letting *love* in—can feel overwhelming and even terrifying.

In active addiction, we wear a mask. We build walls. And we don't let people get too close because deep down, we're afraid that if they really knew us, they'd walk away.

But recovery lifts the veil. And suddenly, we're face-to-face with a world that's been waiting for us to come alive again. A world full of people, opportunities, relationships, and connection—and yet, we stand there, uncertain and unsteady, like toddlers learning to walk. That's where the love languages come in.

The 5 Love Languages is a concept developed by Dr. Gary Chapman that helps us understand different ways people express and receive love. In recovery, this can be especially important because many of us are learning—sometimes for the first time—how to build healthy, loving relationships without the barriers of shame, guilt, or past hurt. Understanding these love languages allows us to connect more deeply with our partners, family, friends, and even ourselves.

Dr. Chapman has identified these five love languages: Words of Affirmation, Quality Time, Receiving Gifts, Physical Touch, and Acts of Service. It's possible to give and receive love using any of these languages, but it is important to be aware of each of them, as we all tend to have a primary language through which we feel love. While you might feel love more impactfully when you receive a gift from someone, I might feel more love when someone verbally compliments me.

Let's dig in and take a look at each love language, and as we do, let's explore how each love language applies to recovery—how we receive love and, just as importantly, how we can give and practically apply love to our everyday interactions. Because love isn't one-sided. And healing requires both give and take.

As you read, take note of which of the love languages speak to you and those in your life. At the end of this chapter, I've included a link to Dr. Chapman's website. There, you can take a test to discover your love language and dive into so many other resources to learn more.

1. Words of Affirmation

Receiving love through Words of Affirmation:
Hear and accept compliments and encouragement.

In addiction, we often hear words like "failure," "disappointment," or "hopeless." In recovery, new words can fuel us by reminding us we are growing, worthy, loved, and seen.

I remember when someone looked me in the eye and said, "You inspire me." It was like they hugged my soul with those few words. Words of Affirmation is my love language. When others share even a few positive words with me, it brings me great joy and strength. After years of being told what a disappointment I was, hearing positive remarks and accepting compliments was awkward. Maybe you can relate. When you're used to shame, grace feels unfamiliar—but it's exactly what I needed at such a pivotal time in my life.

Giving love through Words of Affirmation: Share compliments and encouragement with others.

We can empower someone with Words of Affirmation by speaking life into someone's soul. Tell your friend, "I see how hard you're working." Celebrate small milestones. Your effort doesn't have to be a grand gesture. It can be as simple as sending a short text or card to someone working hard that states, "You are doing a good job. I'm proud of you— keep going." You would be surprised how a few simple words can change someone's day—or really, change the trajectory of their entire life.

2. Quality Time

Receiving love through Quality Time: Accept and be grateful for the time others share with you.

Addiction isolates, but recovery reconnects. Spending time with someone without distraction says, "You matter to me."

The times I've felt the most loved weren't during fancy celebrations—they were in quiet coffee shop talks, walks after meetings, or just sitting in silence while holding space for each other. I remember my husband taking me to dinner when I had just returned home from inpatient treatment. He was balancing a lot so I could seek long-term care. He worked all hours of the day and constantly had to be on his phone. At dinner, I asked if he needed to be on a call, and he replied, "I left my phone at home so we could spend time with no interruptions." After so many years of feeling like I was at the bottom of the totem pole in our home, that let me know he was intentional about both of us making changes moving forward.

Giving love through Quality Time: Intentionally share your time with another while giving them your undivided attention.

Giving your time and being fully present can mean putting down your phone, leaving your smartwatch on the dresser, and getting lost in conversation. As you recover, maybe you aren't ready for deep conversations yet. Start small. Plan an activity such as going to a show or taking a walk. Quality Time can also be as simple as asking someone how their day was and then really listening. Allow your eyes to meet theirs and acknowledge their words. When we show up consistently, it tells people, "I'm here, and I'm not going anywhere—you can count on me."

3. Receiving Gifts

Receiving love through Receiving Gifts: Accept gifts with a grateful heart.

In recovery, gifts can be powerful reminders that we matter. A gift given in love can touch deep places in the heart and encourage us to keep going.

I still have small gifts people have given me over the years. Receiving and cherishing them reminds me that I mattered enough for someone to go out of their way for me. A coworker I had difficulty connecting with once brought me a small jar called Kintsugi. Kintsugi is a Japanese art form where broken pottery is repaired using gold or silver lacquer. Instead of hiding the cracks, it highlights them, turning the damage into something beautiful and symbolizing how brokenness and healing can create a stronger, more valuable whole. The pottery was her way of saying, "I see you; you aren't broken, you are beautiful." Her gift opened a new friendship and a stronger work relationship.

Giving love through Receiving (Giving) Gifts:
When someone else's love language is Receiving
Gifts, you can show your love by giving them a
heartfelt gift.

Gifts for someone in recovery (or anyone) do not
have to be expensive or even cost anything—a
sobriety token, a handwritten note, or a devotional
book. Writing a note of encouragement to someone
whose love language is Receiving Gifts can be just
what they need to get through the day. Create a
care package for a loved one in early sobriety with
a few trinkets, then leave it for them to find. Share
a bookmark with a verse that meant something to
you. These tokens can create beautiful connection
and good feelings, the memories of which will last a
lifetime.

4. Physical Touch

Receiving love through Physical Touch: A trusted individual's safe and welcomed touch is the most impactful way for some people to experience love.

For many in recovery, however, physical touch is complicated due to trauma or abuse. This was the case for me. I experienced major intimacy issues after having been in several abusive relationships. When the drugs and alcohol were no longer a part of my life, I had to become re-acclimated to my response to Physical Touch. Counseling helped, but so did taking baby steps, allowing loved ones to approach me with safe, non-sexual, appropriate touch. A hug after a milestone and a hand on the shoulder during a prayer felt safe and helped me eventually shift into a life where physical touch became welcomed.

I didn't realize how much I needed a hug until a loved one offered it—genuine love with no strings attached.

Giving love through Physical Touch: Touch, when approached respectfully, can help someone experience love and acceptance.

While we must respect boundaries when it comes to touch, don't underestimate the healing power touch holds. Offer a hug when it's welcomed. High-five or fist-bump someone to acknowledge an accomplishment. Put your hand on their shoulder as you pray with others, but always ask first. Touch and being respectful of touch can remind people they're seen, known, and cared for. For those whose primary love language is Physical Touch, someone reaching out to them can radiate their entire being. My youngest child literally melts in my arms when I stop what I'm doing and give a "for no particular reason" hug.

5. Acts of Service

Receiving love through Acts of Service: Allowing others to do something for you can mean allowing them to love you.

Recovery requires accepting help, especially at the beginning. Sometimes, the biggest act of love someone can offer is showing up—providing a ride, bringing food, or being present during court proceedings. These moments speak louder than words to the recipient whose love language is Acts of Service. Balancing daily tasks while getting acclimated to a recovery program can be overwhelming. Imagine allowing someone to step in and help with a task just because they want to show their love. Accepting Acts of Service is a cornerstone of unity in recovery.

When someone gave up their time to support me by giving me rides to recovery meetings without expecting anything in return, it took a burden off my shoulders that I am still grateful for to this day and was important in reminding me that unconditional love exists.

Giving love through Acts of Service: Doing something for someone out of the kindness of your heart is a beautiful picture of brotherly love.

You don't need to be a therapist or a sponsor to serve others. Bring someone coffee before a meeting. Offer to babysit so they can attend recovery group, take an uninterrupted shower, or have space for quiet time to stay grounded in their recovery program. Offer to run some errands for them or help with things around the house to lighten their load. Love is action, not just feeling.

Learning about and putting into practice *The 5 Love Languages* has helped me build bridges back to my marriage, my children, my community, my self-worth, and ultimately to God. Love isn't just a word we say in recovery; it's how we live. And when we learn to receive and give love, we begin to restore what addiction tried to destroy.

So, I'll ask you this: What is your love language in recovery? And how can you show love to others by becoming aware of and responding to them in their love language? Remember, healing doesn't happen alone. Healing happens when we let love in—and give love out.

As Gary Chapman says, "Love is a choice you make every day."

Love is not something we do to completion. We must choose to love and be loved ongoingly—when it's uncomfortable, risky, and even when we're still healing from everything that told us to build walls instead of bridges.

Real love—the kind that lasts and upholds us—isn't perfect. It doesn't always sound right or feel easy. It shows up when you're learning. It holds space when you need to figure things out. It doesn't walk away when you get it wrong. Love is a learned language, and healing is part of learning it. By loving and being loved, you can learn how to stay open, trust, and believe you are worth loving. Know that the people walking alongside you are learning, too. Some days, you'll get it right, and some days you won't. But that doesn't mean you are failing. It just means you are growing and making progress.

Give yourself time. Give others grace. Love is a new language we must learn to speak as we recover—one built on truth, hope, and second chances. Keep choosing love and keep letting love choose you—every day.

Reflection

Learning to give and receive love is a lot like learning a new language. In the beginning, it feels awkward and unfamiliar, and we're bound to stumble along the way. But with time, practice, and patience, it starts to feel more natural. Gary Chapman's The 5 Love Languages *is a valuable guide—not only for those in recovery but also for the people who love and support them.*

Addiction distorts and even silences love, but recovery invites us to experience it in its purest form—through kind words, helpful actions, humble gifts, shared time, and safe, healing touch. These aren't just ways to build or rebuild relationships; they can also help restore the broken places within us.

For those in recovery, understanding your love language helps you accept care without fear. And for loved ones, it creates a path to connect with more compassion.

> *What love language did you most naturally gravitate to when reading this? When was the last time you fully accepted love without wondering if you deserved it? Are you offering love in a way others can truly receive it?*

To learn more about *The 5 Love Languages* and discover the many opportunities Dr. Gary Chapman and his team have to offer, visit: www.5lovelanguages.com.

CHAPTER TEN

God...Can You Hear Me?

"Our prayers may be awkward. Our attempts may be feeble. But since the power of prayer is in the One who hears it and not in the one who says it, our prayers do make a difference."
—Max Lucado

A s I started walking my path to sobriety, I quickly learned the importance of being in unity with my Higher Power. There was one problem: I had no idea how to talk to God. Maybe you can relate?

I prayed as I'd heard others and as I thought I should, but it felt awkward. I was unsure if I was doing it right, almost like at the beginning stages of dating someone. That may sound silly. But if you think about it, building a relationship with God isn't so different from building a relationship with anyone else, so feeling awkward as you maneuver through learning to communicate with Him isn't silly at all.

Some of my deepest, most authentic talks with God have occurred when I've been in places you may think He wouldn't be tuned into me—the closet in my bedroom, the car as I'm driving to work, the shower, waiting in a fast-food drive-through line, sitting at my desk, and in my kitchen while cooking. My point is that we can talk to God anytime from anywhere. And whether we speak out loud or think thoughts directed toward Him, I can assure you He hears our innermost thoughts and desires.

I used to say out loud, "God... can You hear me?" I would awkwardly introduce myself as if He didn't already know me. Eventually, I learned there is no wrong way to talk to God, though I certainly no longer feel the need to introduce myself to Him. Most of the time, I prefer to say prayers out loud, which eases my fears that I will not be heard. But whether we speak out loud, in our hearts, with pre-written words, using our own sentiments, or just crying out in joy or anguish, God hears us.

Early on in my sobriety, I chose a few pre-written prayers that spoke to me and made it a practice to say them at different times throughout the day. At first, I set reminders, but eventually, saying the prayers became part of my daily routine.

For example, before my feet even hit the floor each day, I say my morning prayer. Before I eat lunch, I say the Lord's Prayer. Essentially, I picked times throughout the day when I could attach a prayer to a recurring event so I wouldn't forget. I have found that praying throughout my day keeps me grounded. Having set times to pray reminds me to take a brief timeout from my busy schedule to reset. This helps ensure I am still connected to my Higher Power, not attempting to make my way through the day with my own will and ego.

I'm including some of my favorite prayers that have brought me through "one day at a time." I hope they will also lead you to peace and comfort. Oh, and you should know that I say special prayers for all my friends each day—it's just another way that God is creating unity between you and me. Long after you have closed the pages of this book, we will be connected through prayer for years to come.

Serenity Prayer

God, grant me the serenity to accept the things I cannot change,
the courage to change the things I can,
and the wisdom to know the difference. Amen.

The Lord's Prayer

Our Father, Who art in heaven, hallowed be Thy name;
Thy kingdom come; Thy will be done on earth as it is in heaven.
Give us this day our daily bread;
and forgive us our trespasses
as we forgive those who trespass against us;
and lead us not into temptation but deliver us from evil. Amen.

Guardian Angel Prayer

Angel of God, my guardian dear,
to Whom His love commits me here.
Ever this day be at my side
to light and guard to rule and guide. Amen.

Prayer for Courage to Connect

Lord, give me the courage to extend my hand
and heart to others with love,
even when it's hard to do so.
Help me see their needs
and respond with compassion and understanding. Amen

A Prayer for Unity

Lord, Let Your love burn away all division within us.
Heal what separates hearts, and mend what pride has broken.
Unite us in Your mercy, so we may see one another not as strangers,
but as brothers and sisters, each one a reflection of You.
Pour out the light of compassion into every corner of our world.
Let it begin with me. Amen.

The Fiat of the Eternal Father (Morning Prayer)

My beloved Father, thy will be done on Earth as it is in Heaven.
Be thou my Father. Be always my Eternal Father.
Do not leave my soul. Do not abandon me.
Do not leave me out of your sight, my Father,
for I am your child whom You have created
to please You, to adore You, to honor You,
living my days as You have given me the license to live it. Amen.

Prayer for Daily Neglects (Evening Prayer)

My God, who unceasingly calls us to union with You,
I ask You to pardon my daily neglects
when I ignored and rejected this call
and to make me love You more,
so that I never miss Your offer to grow in holiness. Amen.

A Prayer for Surrender and Clarity

God, I come to You with a willing heart.
Please forgive me for the wrongs I've done,
the things I see,
and the things I've yet to understand.

Help me to see my part in every situation,
not to shame myself, but to grow.
Clear away the pride and fear that cloud my vision.

Make me usable.
Mold me into someone who brings peace, not chaos.
I turn my will and my life over to You today.

Guide my thoughts, my words, and my actions.
Let me be a light, even in places I once brought darkness.

Thank You for loving me through it all.
I surrender everything to You.

I trust in you. Amen.

CHAPTER ELEVEN

Note to Self...

"Fill your paper with the breathings of your heart."
— *William Wordsworth*

E mbracing unity as we recover is crucial to our progress—this is why I continually step out and tell my story. I've had to fight for the wisdom I've gained, and it is my honor to share it with others. No matter where you are on your path, you have the power to significantly impact the recovery community by bravely and humbly sharing your experiences. Telling your story begins with finding the right words.

Over the years, I have been encouraged to put my thoughts into writing. I was always resistant to the suggestion of placing what was on my mind on paper. I would try at times, but never with serious effort. I didn't realize that writing would help me untangle my thoughts, allowing me to process difficult events and turn them into future victories.

For much of my recovery, journaling sounded boring and maybe even scary. I would think, *Why would I want to write down things that could be found and possibly used against me?* You have to remember that I was an addict for a long period of my life—decades! All of my thoughts, secrets, guilt, and shame were to be tucked away or masked, certainly not written about.

Looking back, I believe my resistance to journaling was actually about the fear of not being ready to connect with my reality. I clung to my denial, and in an extremely dysfunctional way, I protected myself from feeling the things I needed to in order to grow because, as you and I could probably agree, growth is hard work.

I felt crippled by fear that I wasn't smart enough to write anything. I would try, but end up telling myself, *You aren't doing this right.* Then, I would either crumple the page or tuck my notebook away in a sock drawer so I didn't have to look at it anymore. But the suggestion always came back up that I should try journaling. And so, the cycle of not really trying and then talking myself out of it would begin again... and again... and again for several years.

When I started inpatient treatment at a dual-diagnosis treatment facility, journaling became an assignment. Homework, if you will. I was required to write just a few thoughts each night to share with my treatment counselors. The task was daunting, but I did each assignment as instructed. At that point in my life, I was finally ready to do whatever it took to heal—yes, even submit to writing.

And you know what? I quickly found that it wasn't as scary or as overwhelming as I had imagined. I saw almost instantly that writing just a few jumbled thoughts could open a window of dialogue with myself. It helped me identify things I could share with my counselors, in group sessions, and during recovery meetings. I also discovered that discussing what I had written led to conversations that helped me process my thoughts and also helped others process their own thoughts.

By opening a window to my mind through journaling, a window to my soul was opened simultaneously. And that touched the souls of others. Witnessing this transfer of love caught my attention and motivated me to keep going—and to keep journaling.

You may have heard or read about how the little things can add up to big things. Baby steps can make the biggest impact on your life. My writing journey began with a pen and a scratch piece of paper that said, "Note to Self." I quickly discovered that journaling is a baby step that can lead to bigger things. For example, look at my story— I was a woman who didn't have time for some silly idea of putting my thoughts on paper; now, I have written several books to share hope with you! I have used some of my journal notes from over the years to create articles for *Voice of Truth* magazine for my column, Recovery Reflections, and fuel the encouragement I share on social media. Those "Notes to Self" have turned into a lamp to light the path for others!

There are many other ways journaling has strengthened my life. Here are just a few examples for you to consider. Journaling can:

- Provide a way to focus on goals
- Help identify triggers
- Track progress and growth
- Improve self-confidence
- Lessen feelings of anxiety and reduce stress
- Inspire ideas & open reflection
- Encourage self-love
- Eliminate negative self-talk
- Initiate growth toward emotional awareness

Because connection is the opposite of addiction, as we work to eliminate substance use, we must also strive to connect with others and, most importantly, connect with ourselves. None of this is easy. But we aren't promised easy. What we are promised in recovery is that, with consistency and honest effort, we will find a better way of life.

Perhaps the first step to that better way of life for you includes a pen and a few pages of paper to jot down some thoughts. I've added some pages in this book so you can give it a try. I've titled the pages like I did for my first journaling efforts: "Note to Self."

Start small. Maybe something from this book stood out that you can relate to? Write it down and open that proverbial window I just mentioned. Perhaps you prefer expressing yourself with drawing? It doesn't have to be perfect—use stick figures if necessary. I am always reminding myself that the goal is "Progress, not perfection." I constantly give this grace to myself when trying something new. This attitude gives me permission to focus on smaller achievements instead of the end goal, which is far less overwhelming.

The point is to put pen to paper and see what comes from within. While you are bravely giving it a try, whether it's in print, cursive, shorthand, spelled correctly or not, remember, you are not alone. I'm most likely sitting somewhere in this world doing the same thing, thinking of you—praying for your courage and strength—one day at a time.

Note to Self:

You are taking the first steps in healing! Keep going! Let this be the place where your truth feels safe and grace is present.

Note to Self:

....

....

....

....

....

....

....

....

....

....

....

....

....

....

....

....

....

The window to your mind and soul is opening!
Keep going, keep growing, keep writing!

Note to Self:

If you get stuck, write down a few things that you are grateful for.
Gratitude invites opportunities for growth!

Note to Self:

....

....

....

....

....

....

....

....

....

....

....

....

....

....

....

....

....

....

....

This space is safe—express emotions without worry of being judged.
You are making wonderful progress!

Note to Self:

....

....

....

....

....

....

....

....

....

....

....

....

....

....

....

Even a single sentence can lighten a heavy heart.
Keep going! You are doing it!

Note to Self:

....

....

....

....

....

....

....

....

....

....

....

....

....

....

....

....

....

....

List things you would like to discover on your recovery path.
This is a safe space; keep writing it out.

Note to Self:

Life on life's terms can hit hard sometimes. By writing it down, you are letting it out and making room for new things.

Note to Self:

....

....

....

....

....

....

....

....

....

....

....

....

....

....

....

....

....

....

One day, you'll look back and see how far you've come—one day at a time, one page at a time. I am proud of you!

CHAPTER TWELVE

Let's Stay Connected!

"Only through our connectedness to others can we really know
and enhance the self. And only through working on the self can
we begin to enhance our connectedness to others."
—Harriet Goldhor Lerner

A s you come to the end of this book, I invite you to lean into your progress. You are fortunate if you are in recovery or if you are just beginning to look at the possibilities that ditching the drink or drug might bring. Whether you are just starting out or have been on the recovery path for years, connecting with others who are or have been where you are is crucial.

Today is a good day to recover. One reason is that there is a movement of social justice for breaking the stigma of addiction that you and I, my friend, are right in the middle of. The days of secret meetings and having code words for 12-step programs and anonymity are shifting. You may hear the argument from people with long-term sobriety that recovering behind closed doors worked for them for decades, so why alter the process?

There are several reasons for the shift. A few main factors come to the forefront each time I dive into this complex, worldwide transition. Simply put, the social impacts of the COVID-19 pandemic left millions of people yearning to have a voice, and technology has made having that voice possible. With suicide and overdose rates at an all-time high, people are uniting across the globe to bring awareness. In a few short years, this has created a recovery world unlike anything we have ever witnessed before.

Today's technology allows information to flow at lightning speeds. Social media may have its drawbacks in some areas; however, for the intent and purpose of creating unity and connecting people across the globe to bolster recovery from addiction, planting it within social media has allowed it to bloom exponentially.

Recovery pages on social media offer connection with a reach far greater than we may find with in-person meetings. I've met some of my closest friends in recovery online and through social networking. Please do not misunderstand my message: I couldn't imagine my recovery path without "the rooms of recovery." (If you are new to recovery, that is lingo for actively participating in 12-step recovery programs such as Alcoholics Anonymous, Celebrate Recovery, or Al-Anon, just to name a few.) These rooms have played a very important role in my recovery and could in yours, too.

My point, though, is to share that, in my experience, I have found that having a balance of both in-person meetings and online connections is very beneficial. The options for unity on these social pages are endless and offer connections to people you wouldn't be able to meet locally.

My social page, Sober-Now, delivers inspirational messages and connections to other pages for live events and podcasts. Podcasts are an excellent resource for many in recovery from addiction. Usually posted on a weekly or monthly basis, these online, radio-like conversations can be accessed from home, while in the car, grocery shopping, taking a walk, or anywhere you have time to listen.

Most podcasters post their content across several different platforms, allowing the option to view the podcast either prerecorded or as it is live-streamed. Several recovery-related podcasts are hosted by people who have experienced addiction firsthand. These podcasters share impactful information and the valuable lessons they have learned along their journey through recovery. Many podcasters even give their listeners an opportunity to be guests and share their stories, offering hope and inspiration to others.

I cannot begin to count the times in early sobriety that I needed to hit a meeting when none were available. Today, when I feel the urge for connection and am unable to attend a meeting, I use my phone or laptop and find a podcast to help me process whatever emotion I am experiencing with my recovery. I can scroll through the topics and descriptions until I discover one specific to the need that has reared its head and even threatened to derail my progress.

I find great inspiration in the thousands of episodes available at any given time. I'm grateful for the rigorous hours of work podcasters spend on creating these programs and the brave individuals who recover out loud by sharing their testimonies.

Listed in the next few pages are some of the recovery-related podcasts that I have found to be beneficial to my daily life. Each of these podcasts has several episodes available online, accessible to anyone at any time. I have even included a sober book club and a sober library, in case you are interested in staying up to date with some of the best recovery books out there, as well as a publisher with many inspirational, bestselling books to add to your reading list.

In addition, you will find ways to connect with some of the ministries I belong to or follow. Many of these meet online, offering prayer gatherings and leadership connection meetings that inspire you to tap into your purpose and provide opportunities to share your personal experiences! These groups have offered much growth on my own path, and I have witnessed the same for countless others in the process. Take a minute to browse through some of what they offer; you might just encounter the unity your heart has been searching for.

When the first book in the *I'm Sober...So Now What?* series launched, I was extremely fortunate to connect with several of these platforms to share my message of hope. The opportunity to spend time with them has created connections worldwide. I encourage you to give them a try. Who knows? You may even find me there. Nothing brings me more joy than knowing that once you close the pages of this book, we will be able to stay connected through some of these valuable resources.

Resources for Support – Help is always available:

Alcoholics Anonymous

*A free, anonymous, nonprofit organization
that uses a 12-step program to help individuals achieve and
maintain sobriety from alcohol.*

www.aa.org

1-800-839-1686

Find a meeting: www.aa-meetings.com

Al-Anon/Alateen

*Support groups for those affected by someone else's drinking.
Al-Anon is for adults who have a loved one with an alcohol problem,
while Alateen is specifically for teenagers in similar situations.*

www.al-anon.org

1-888-4AL-ANON (1-888-425-2666)

Narcotics Anonymous

*A free, anonymous, nonprofit organization
that uses a 12-step program to help individuals achieve and
maintain sobriety from drugs.*

www.na.org

1-818-773-9999

Celebrate Recovery

A free, anonymous, Christian-based, 12-step program that offers support and resources for individuals seeking sobriety and freedom from addictive behaviors and other life issues.

www.celebraterecovery.com

Find a meeting: www.crlocator.com

National Suicide Prevention Hotline

www.988lifeline.org

1-800-273-8255

24-hour access: text/call 988

Find a Treatment Center Near You:

Substance Abuse and Mental Health Services Administration (SAMHSA)

www.findtreatment.gov or www.samhsa.gov

1-800-662-HELP (1-800-622-4357)

Scan the QR Code for my social media pages, podcasts, and
to pay it forward; or visit: www.linktr.ee/sobernow
Would you like me to speak to your group?
Email: Melissa@Sober-Now.com

Sober-Now is a non-profit conceived through the publishing of
the *I'm Sober...So Now What?* book series. It became clear early on
that many people need a message of hope, especially those in places
where hope is hard to come by. Through generous donations,
Sober-Now has sent thousands of free copies of the book series to
people in treatment facilities, jails, human trafficking safe houses,
shelters, and recovery groups worldwide. Connecting with others
is a beautiful blessing that allows us to offer a lifeline to those in
recovery searching for a better way of life.

The Hope Shot is a community recovery organization dedicated to helping individuals overcome substance misuse and lead fulfilling lives in recovery. They provide peer support, resources, and a safe space for people on their path to recovery, connecting them with the support they need to thrive. Find out what The Hope Shot has to offer by scanning their QR code.

Women World Leaders is a global ministry that empowers women to walk in their God-given purpose. Through the unity of fellowship, WWL inspires women to develop their gifts and experience the joy of partnering with God in His glorious work. Find out more at: womenworldleaders.com

Voice of Truth is a full-color magazine written and designed by women from around the world that empowers readers to walk in their God-given purpose, grow in sisterhood, and experience the joy of God's creation. Past editions of the magazine are available digitally; future editions will be available in print. Visit: womenworldleaders.com

United Men of Honor is a program designed to empower and support men in their personal growth and development. It aims to create a community of like-minded individuals committed to living with integrity, purpose, and honor. The program provides resources, guidance, and mentorship to help men navigate challenges and cultivate positive change in their lives. Visit: unitedmenofhonor.com

World Publishing and Productions is on mission to empower you to share your God story with the world. They offer one-on-one coaching, editing, and a complete publishing experience. Iron sharpens iron (Proverbs 27:17), and God has gifted us each with unique gifts and stories meant to be shared. Find more information, along with impactful and inspiring books, on their website: worldpublishingandproductions.com

Visit some of my online friends below and find out why they are a wonderful go-to for staying connected through online recovery!

Benjamin Lerner
Benjaminlerner.com

Letsrecover2gether.com

IG: sober.book.club

Are you ready for the next book in the
I'm Sober... So Now What? series?

COMING SOON

Stay sober and stay tuned...